WITHDRAWN

Dr. John V. Van Sickle has been chairman of
the Department of Economics at Vanderbilt
University, at Wabash College, and at the
University of the Americas in Mexico. Executive Secretary of the Principles of Freedom
Committee, Dr. Van Sickle is the author of
Direct Taxation in Austria and a co-author
with Benjamin A. Rogge of a college textbook, *Introduction to Economics*.

FREEDOM IN JEOPARDY

John V. Van Sickle

FREEDOM IN JEOPARDY

The Tyranny of Idealism

THE WORLD PUBLISHING COMPANY
NEW YORK AND CLEVELAND

Published by The World Publishing Company
2231 West 110th Street, Cleveland, Ohio 44102
Published simultaneously in Canada by
Nelson, Foster & Scott Ltd.

First Printing—April, 1969

Manufactured at World Publishing Press,
a division of The World Publishing Company,
Cleveland, Ohio

Library of Congress Catalog Card Number: 68–54126

PRINTED IN THE UNITED STATES OF AMERICA

WORLD PUBLISHING
TIMES MIRROR

This volume is a publication of
The Principles of Freedom Committee

Contents

Foreword

THIS BOOK GROWS out of lectures given several years ago at Union College (Barbourville, Kentucky) and at the University of the Americas, in Mexico City. It has benefited from the vigorous reactions of students and from helpful suggestions by Professors Ben A. Rogge, Warren Nutter, and Milton Friedman. Anyone familiar with the writings of Ludwig von Mises and Friedrich A. Hayek will recognize my indebtedness to them.

My thesis is very simple. It may help the reader to follow the argument in support of this thesis if I summarize it at this point.

Man is an imperfect creature; a mixture of saint and sinner; sometimes bold, sometimes timid; at one moment unbelievably generous, at another incredibly ruthless; sometimes rational, at other times naively credulous; a believer in myths and miracles. Through a long and almost miraculous concatenation

ix

of circumstances (beautifully sketched out by Louis Rougier, the eminent French philosopher, in an article in *La Revue des Deux Mondes* and subsequently expanded into what hopefully will soon appear in English under the title *The Genius of the West*), the slow triumph of the rational in this imperfect man has at long last given him powers over nature so vast as to make possible in our own time and in most parts of the world the abolition of anything we would today call poverty.

This man is not a rugged individualist. He is a social animal, a joiner. He strives to realize most of his hopes and to ward off most of his fears through group action. In the West, at least, he has discovered three social institutions (the rule of law, federalism, and the market or the free enterprise system) that will make it possible, if he but develops them further, for him to put an end to group warfare and to live in peace and harmony with his fellows. If he fails in this greatest endeavor, it will be due, I am persuaded, less to his numerous imperfections than to a noble imperfection—to a generous and impatient compassion that leads him to place too much reliance on the ways of coercion and too little on the ways of persuasion.

I shall be very critical of most of the coercive welfare measures of the last third of a century that his compassion has led him to support. I want to make it clear at the outset, therefore, that my strictures will be directed not at the ends—for the most part they are ends I share—but at the means. These means, though reminiscent of those popular three hundred years ago (in the age of mercantilism), are currently described as liberal. I have been urged to label as conservative those I shall recommend. But this would clearly be a misnomer since they call for the repeal of most of the interventions modern liberals applaud. *Radical* would be a more descriptive term, for if I am correct the means I recommend would get at the roots of the troubles that now threaten the foundations of the unique civilization described by Professor Rougier.

Yet these recommendations are not radical in the sense of being new. My generation, the pre-World War I generation, would have called them liberal, as English-speaking peoples outside the United States still do. I have insisted, therefore— and perhaps inadvisably—on keeping the old words *liberal* and *liberalism*, with their generous faith in voluntarism, but I capitalize the first letters when I use them in their original and traditional sense. In the battle for men's minds these words are too valuable to be given up to those who would take us back to the age of mercantilism.

The first six chapters deal with the way in which people, as members of groups, reach decisions, and explain why these decisions must satisfy the rule of law, the federal principle, and the market's adjustment mechanism if they are not to jeopardize liberty.

The next six chapters describe a number of recent welfare measures that are the products of group decisions, of the political processes of decision making. It is clear now that these measures failed in their generous purposes. They have made it impossible for many of the most hapless to find work; they have weakened the decentralizing and equalizing forces in the free enterprise system; they have reduced incentives and retarded growth; and they have repeatedly overridden the wishes of local majorities, thereby inviting disrespect for law in general and alarmingly heightening regional, occupational, and ethnic tensions.

I shall argue that these unwanted and unfortunate results are due in considerable part to the fact that the measures reviewed have been directed at helping rich and poor alike in overcrowded occupations, instead of helping individuals in actual need to shift themselves and their resources into occupations where rewards are higher and where their usefulness to their fellows would be greater.

It will be further argued that these measures have jeopardized the personal freedom to which liberals of all persuasions are attached because: (a) they have violated the rule of law, not as modern legal scholars conceive the term, but as it came down to us through Greece, Rome, the medieval Christian Church, and English philosophers such as John Locke, and as the Fathers of the American Constitution understood it; (b) they have disregarded the federal principle, with its commitment to tolerance and its insistence that the will of local majorities should not be overridden by a national majority except in matters clearly assigned to the central government in the original compact of union or subsequently assigned to it through the formal amending process; and (c) they have reduced the market's capacity to perform its major function, that of making it worthwhile for millions of people to specialize and to cooperate with one another without central direction and without that degree of unanimity required whenever actions have to rest on decisions reached through the political processes. In a popular democracy, members of minority groups are likely to be ill served through the political processes of decision making since these will necessarily reflect majority wishes and prejudices.

In all societies of which we have any record the majority looks askance at extreme inequalities and will, if it can, strive to reduce them. Capitalism is at once a powerful destroyer of old inequalities and a creator of new ones. It can never produce anything approaching complete equality. The more competitive it is, however, the more certain it is that the inequalities it produces will be functionally justified and hence socially and politically acceptable to a public that understands its *modus operandi*. It would seem the better part of wisdom, therefore, for the state to encourage competition. I am not arguing that the rewards that would flow from a genuinely competitive capitalism must be regarded as sacrosanct. On the contrary, I share the prevailing egalitarian bias and contend that there is a Liberal way to reduce inequalities that is consistent with the rule of law and the federal principle and that would interfere so little with the market's adjustment mechanism and its rewards and penalties as, on balance, to improve the capitalistic performance. The question is whether the political processes can discover this Liberal way and be prevented from carrying equalization too far.

With the wisdom of hindsight, it is easy now to suggest a reallocation of functions between the central government and the state governments in which the central government's sole responsibility in the welfare field would be that of seeing to it that no one's income fell below some modest minimum. Capitalism is so incredibly productive that it could support such a commitment.

There are a number of ways of carrying out this undertaking. The negative income-tax method first suggested by Professor Milton Friedman, of the University of Chicago, some ten years ago has won wide acceptance. It is technically simple. Families declaring incomes below some specified amount would be given cash rebates. As a family's earned income rose, the rebate would decline by lesser amounts until it reached zero. Beyond this level all families would be expected to pay a positive income tax.

This method meets two of the tests suggested in this book: consistency with the rule of law and consistency with the operating requirements of the private enterprise system. It would be disastrous if the negative income tax were added to the existing welfare measures. It would be economical, however, if, as Friedman insisted, it replaced what he called the present "ragbag" of welfare measures. And it could easily become the means of strengthening the federal principle if it were part of a package deal involving: (a) the explicit exclusion of the central government from all welfare functions other than that connected with the negative income tax, and (b) the equally explicit requirement that the central government share its revenues as a matter of right with the states, in accordance with a formula that would deprive it of all discretion and hence of the formidable power to dictate to the states, which existing sharing devices now give it (matching grants-in-aid and direct project supports of a bewildering variety).

The proposal is radical and risky. But timid remedies will not meet the crisis now confronting this country. In a note in the Appendix (p. 176) additional constitutional safeguards are suggested that would, in my judgment, so reduce the risks as to justify the experiment. If the experiment succeeded, belief in capitalism and federalism would be restored. Neither system is perfect. At best they are means, not ends. But capitalism is the only way of getting people to cooperate that has until now demonstrated both its compatibility with liberty and its capacity to abolish poverty. And federalism is the only way so far discovered of dividing sovereignty that is capable of reconciling local loyalties with the larger loyalty we call nationalism.

In a world where men are neither very wise nor very virtuous, capitalism and federalism may be the only means now available for preventing the tyranny of idealism from destroying freedom. They may also provide the only means now available for protecting the liberty and the dignity of the individual and for bringing peace and some modest degree of comfort to a troubled and divided world.

FREEDOM IN JEOPARDY

1

Freedom
and the State

THESE ARE EXCITING TIMES. A scientific revolution is in full
course. It has already given us the technical power to make
life on this earth a heaven or hell. This power is largely in the
hands of national states. Will they use it to destroy the world?
Will they surrender it to a world government? I hope that they
will not do the first; I doubt strongly that they will do the
second. National states will be with us for a long time to come[1]
because they are still needed to carry out what a distinguished
social anthropologist and ardent internationalist called "the
very business of culture."[2] The danger is not so much that they
will destroy the world as that they will destroy liberty.

Can national states both keep the peace and protect liberty?
The dilemma is real. The maintenance of domestic peace requires the existence of national states with a monopoly of the
power to use violence. The maintenance of liberty requires
that this power be used moderately. But if, as Lord Acton

claimed, "power tends to corrupt, and absolute power corrupts absolutely,"[3] can men wielding absolute power use it moderately? This is a problem political philosophers have wrestled with through the centuries. It was *the* central issue at a gathering in Philadelphia 180 years ago. The answer hammered out there will be described presently.

But first something needs to be said about liberty itself. What is it? Why is it important? Is it threatened, and if so, why?

· ON LIBERTY ·

What is liberty? Abraham Lincoln's definition will do as a starting point:

> With some the word liberty may mean for each man to do as he pleases with himself and the products of his labor; while with others the same word may mean for some men to do as they please with other men and the products of other men's labor. Here are two, not only different, but incompatible things, called by the same name, liberty. And it follows that each of the things is, by the respective parties, called by two different and incompatible names, liberty and tyranny.[4]

Actually the term, as used today, covers not only the individual liberty Lincoln was concerned with, but an entirely different concept, collective liberty, or the freedom of a group from alien control.[5] All over the world subject peoples have gained freedom in the collective sense, only to see freedom in the individual sense drastically reduced.

Marx's definition. Freedom in the collective sense is important. My concern here, however, is with freedom in the individual sense. Even so circumscribed, the range of views is wide. Karl Marx equated freedom with complete independence.

A being does not regard himself as independent unless he is his own master and he is only his own master when he owes his existence only to himself. A man who lives by the favor of another considers himself a dependent being.[6]

The realm of freedom does not commence until the point is passed where labor, under compulsion of necessity . . . is required.[7]

Freedom, according to this definition, would be possible only when specialization was no longer necessary, when "I can do one thing today and another tomorrow . . . hunt in the morning, fish in the afternoon, work in the evening, criticize after dinner, just as I have a mind, without ever becoming a hunter, a fisherman, shepherd or critic."[8]

Here Marx set up two unattainable and contradictory conditions. Specialization must go because it alienates man from his fellow man, makes him less than a whole being. And scarcity must also go, for otherwise man must work under compulsion. Yet, as Marx himself recognized, it was through the division of labor that an age of affluence was to be reached. Thus in the *Communist Manifesto* (1848) he admitted that specialization under the guidance of the bourgeoisie had accomplished more miracles in the space of scarcely one hundred years than in all the preceding generations together. This was utopian dreaming of the most dangerous sort. It raised expectations which could not possibly be realized.

Marx recognized this danger when he warned against the forcible overthrow of "bourgeois capitalism" before it had abolished "the curse of scarcity." Otherwise the force behind it would be envy, and

envy, setting itself up as power, is only a camouflaged form of cupidity which reestablishes itself and satisfies itself in a different way. . . . Crude Communism is only the culmination of such envy and leveling down on the basis of a preconceived minimum. How little this abolition of private property represents a genuine appreciation is shown by the abstract negation of the whole world of culture and civilization, and the regression to the unnatural simplicity of the poor and wantless individual who has not only not surpassed private property but has not yet even attained it.[9]

Alternative Definitions. "To do as one pleases, this alone is liberty," is the way T. V. Smith defined liberty in *The Democratic Way of Life.*[10] For F. A. Harper, liberty is "a condition where the person may do whatever he desires, according to his wisdom and his conscience."[11] Personally, I accept F. A. von Hayek's more modest definition: "Freedom is a condition of men in which the coercion of some by others is reduced as much as possible."[12]

How Important is Liberty?

We shall return repeatedly in later chapters to the question of how best to minimize coercion. At this point our interest is in another question. Is liberty all that important? Where does it belong in an individual's hierarchy of values?

One thing is clear. Some degree of freedom is a necessity of life itself. Pavlov, the great Russian experimental psychologist, speaks of "the freedom reflex." If an animal "were not provided with the reflex of protest against boundaries set to its freedom, the smallest obstacle in its path would interfere with the proper fulfillment of its natural functions."[13] Applied to man, this appears to mean that without what Professor Hayek calls "a protected sphere"[14] large enough to give him the feeling that he can make meaningful choices, existence is a living death.

This is a sufficient reason for liberty. It is a condition of life itself. Another reason is that it enables many to live reasonably virtuous lives. Only he who can choose between good and evil, as he sees them, can lay claim to virtue. For a very few the choice between liberty and death may be enough. Most of us, however, need a wider range of choices. A cut in salary for one's convictions is easier to face than a concentration camp or a firing squad.

Still another reason, paradoxical as it may sound, grows out of man's ignorance[15] which increases as the totality of knowledge expands. Benjamin Franklin's grasp of all the wisdom of his times was far greater, relatively, than Albert Einstein's understanding of that of his own day. Our long-run interests are best served by allowing millions of individuals to use the knowledge they do possess, to experiment, and to learn through the greatest teacher of them all—trial and error—provided, of course, they are not allowed to use force or fraud, and are not completely sheltered from the consequences of their mistakes.

Is Liberty in Jeopardy?

A free society does not require that everyone be free. Narrow limits must be placed on the actions of children and of the mentally defective; and there must be a reasonable relationship between the liberties normal adults may enjoy and the responsibilities they will accept. Man has always possessed liberties. Only for brief periods, however, and only in a few places, has he had liberty, or the freedom to do whatever was not specifically prohibited by law or by binding custom.[16]

At the beginning of this century, liberty in this sense was on the march. Today it is in retreat. Man appears increasingly disposed to exchange liberty for privilege. The reason is surely not that man is evil; rather that he is incurably romantic. He is too easily swayed by his emotions. He accepts intentions for realities. He trusts his heart more than his head.[17]

Liberty and Equality

Probably there was never a time when men strove more sincerely to make a better world than they do today, and probably the chances of success were never greater. It is no longer utopian to believe in the possibility of a world where all men can live in peace and moderate comfort.

Nonetheless the immediate prospects are grim. Most of the world's peoples are desperately poor. Even in the United States large numbers, though better fed, clothed, housed, and educated than the poor of earlier times, live under conditions the majority of us would find intolerable. We have largely abolished outright physical misery, in the West at least, but we have not abolished and cannot abolish poverty, because poverty is relative. This does not mean that there is no longer need for concern. All that is suggested here is that the poor, in the relative sense, will always be with us. We should be on our guard, therefore, lest our impatience with injustice, our very idealism, lead us to accept measures which will weaken the foundations on which freedom rests, and, in the process, destroy the system of organizing production which has given us the abundance we now enjoy, and has done it with less inequality than any other system, past or present.[18]

This system of producing and distributing wealth goes by many names: the private enterprise system, the free enterprise system, the profit and loss system, the system of competitive markets. Karl Marx called it capitalism. Today friends and foes alike accept the label Marx gave to the complex institutional arrangements to which he devoted a lifetime of study and which he never really understood. Marx's passionate idealism blinded him to capitalism's practical and prosaic merits even as his idealism concealed from him the inevitable and utopian unreality of the communism that was to replace it.

No thoughtful advocate of capitalism pretends that it is perfect. It can be improved. The poor can be helped. Indeed, I shall argue in Chapter 13 for a more radical way of helping the needy than any of those presently to be examined. But it is above all in the interests of the poor that they be helped in ways that do not cripple the economic system. The poor have more to gain in the short run, and vastly more in the long run, from the way competitive market forces distribute rewards than from any politically determined distribution formula that materially slows down the rate of increase in the national output.

· ON VARIETIES OF LIBERALISM ·

Until recently the position defended in this book would have been called liberal. Today, however, the term has been taken over by those who see in government the main agency for making a better world. Since it is awkward to keep putting qualifying adjectives before the various shades of liberalism, the first letters of the words "liberal" and "liberalism" will be capitalized when and only when they are used in the original sense and, incidentally, as they are still understood on the continent of Europe.

Both types of liberals cherish individual freedom. They differ mainly over the role of government. In general, the Liberalism of the Liberal implies more confidence in the capacity of competitive market forces to produce welfare than does the "liberalism" of the "liberal."

My generation—the pre-World War I generation—undertook to make the world safe for democracy, only to learn of the follies that could be committed in its name. Democracy is a means, not an end; yet without it freedom is impossible. Can the two be reconciled? Alexis de Tocqueville ended his classical study of American democracy (1835) on a note of tempered optimism:

> Looking back now from the end of my task . . . I am full of fears and hopes. I see great dangers which may be warded off and mighty evils which may be avoided or kept in check; and I am ever increasingly confirmed in my belief that for democratic nations to be virtuous and prosperous, it is enough if they will to do so. . . . The nations of our day cannot prevent conditions of equality from spreading in their midst. But it depends upon themselves whether equality is to lead to servitude or freedom, knowledge or barbarism, prosperity or wretchedness.[19]

The future can be no clearer to us than it was to De Tocqueville. Ours is the enormously difficult task of making democracy safe for a world in which men have become dependent on one another as never before, in which the vast majority want to live out their lives at peace with their neighbors, and free in both the individual and the collective sense of the word. Again and again democratic governments have broken down, giving way, first to chaotic disorder and then to tyrannical order. For in the end there must be order. Otherwise, as Shakespeare all too well knew,

> Strength should be lord of imbecility
> And the rude son should strike his father dead:
> Force should be right; or rather right and wrong,
> Between whose endless jar justice resides,
> Should lose their names, and so should justice too.
> Then every thing includes itself in power,
> Power into will, will into appetite[20]

2

Decision Making: The Political Process

MEN ARE JOINERS. From earliest times onward they have banded together for any number of reasons, not the least of which was mutual protection. In doing so, each individual had to recognize wills and interests other than his own. He gave up some elements of freedom in the hope of enjoying other elements of his freedom more effectively. Only a Robinson Crusoe can be completely free. Even Crusoe had some difficult decisions to make, and there is much to be learned by trying to imagine how he decided on the best use of his time, his energy, and the physical resources of his island kingdom. But the political processes of decision making were not involved. Our concern is with the way in which decisions are reached when men join together in groups and act as though animated by a single will.

· GROUPS AND THEIR PURPOSES ·

Groups vary in size, in purposes, and in the resources at their disposal. The greatest difference in groups is between those that are voluntary and those that are compulsory, between those possessing only the power of persuasion and those clothed with the power to compel. Only the state has the power to compel. Consequently, it can outlaw any private group and severely regulate those it permits to exist. Otherwise private groups will multiply. Most individuals will be members of many private groups at any given time and members of very many more over a lifetime. Individuals join together to get things done that they could not do alone. As long as the purposes of the group reflect my purposes, the more likely I am to feel that belonging has increased, not diminished, my freedom. My continued attachment may be so intense that I willingly accept restraints that would seem intolerable to an outsider. I accept the priority of the group's purposes over mine. All I can do is not join those whose purposes do not interest me and try to bring the purposes of those I do join closer to mine.

· DISCOVERING THE COMMON WILL ·

How is the will of a group discovered? There is no single method. Much depends on the group's size, its purposes, and the nature of its membership.

Small Voluntary Groups

Small voluntary groups tend to form around a dominant personality. In them the leadership principle prevails. The "leader" likes to give the impression of "running the show." In fact, he usually consults influential members, gathers impressions, and to a considerable extent senses what the majority want, or at any rate, what they will stand for. He is a dictator, but a limited one, since no one is obligated to join the group or to stay in it. This method of decision making operates in groups as diverse as ladies' garden clubs, small business firms, and the street-corner gangs described by William F. Whyte.[1]

Large Voluntary Groups

The discovery of the area of agreement is more difficult in large groups than in small ones. This is due in part to the tendency of a group as it grows to expand the range of its purposes and in part to increasing difficulties of communication. Discussion under orderly rules of debate, followed by a counting of noses (voting), is one way of discovering the common will. This is the political process of decision making. At this point it is enough to note that it provides all-or-nothing solutions. Those on the losing side get nothing. They must submit or get out. The *right to withdraw* is thus very important, particularly where a matter of conscience is involved. If the majority insist on a line of action I think is wrong, it is my duty to protest in the debate and the vote and then get out if I lose.

Where the advantages of membership are great, the right to withdraw will not be lightly invoked. On matters of minor importance, a man on the losing side will say with complete sincerity that he is satisfied with the outcome since it represents what the majority really want. Nonetheless, the *right to withdraw* and its corollaries, the *right to exclude* and the *right to expel*, are important to the life of a group.

The rights to exclude and to expel can work injustices. Yet they are both essential to the maintenance of group solidarity. The right to choose one's associates is an important part of individual freedom. It can safely be protected so long as those exercising it do not possess monopoly power.[2]

The right to withdraw is particularly important. It makes the members of a group cautious about taking on new functions. The members of a golf club know that the good fellowship of the links will be weakened if the club, as a club, decided to take a stand on foreign aid or on the desirability of making two years of Spanish language study compulsory in the local high school. The narrower a group's purposes the more likely it is that there will be a substantial unanimity of opinion on policy matters. Issues on which the membership is sharply divided will seldom be pushed to a vote. This gives time for the discovery of an acceptable compromise. The right to withdraw promotes both tolerance of minority opinion and the practice of compromise.[3]

Compulsory Groups: The State

The state differs from all voluntary groups in its *de jure* possession of the power to coerce. Large organizations like General Motors, the Ford Foundation, or the United Steel Workers of America possess great power, but it is only the power of persuasion, unless the state, deliberately or by default, allows them to use force.

The state must have the power to coerce and it must have a monopoly of it if it is to discharge its first and primary duty —the maintenance of order. The state must have unlimited power to tax, to spend, to fine, to imprison, and, if necessary, to kill those who break the peace. In brief, it must be able to control the persons and the resources of those within its jurisdiction and to determine who may and who may not enter its jurisdiction. It need not exercise all these powers to their fullest, but they must be available in emergencies.

Obviously these powers are amply sufficient to destroy every vestige of individual liberty, and the danger is ever present that they will be so used. It is inherent in the nature of man. Take at random a thousand adults. A few are leaders, innovators, men of action; the vast majority are followers. These few may be cynical and ruthless or sincerely desirous of helping those around them. Cynical or sincere, they need power to accomplish their purposes, and the surest way of getting it is to organize a private group or join and gain control of an existing one.[4] This search for power animates leaders operating in the private sector no less than in the public sector. As will be noted in Chapter 5, powerful checks automatically come into play when ambitious men seek to use voluntary groups for their own ends, particularly those organized for profits. There are no equally effective checks on men who seek to use the state for their purposes. Consequently there are continuous pressures driving the state to extend its jurisdiction over wider territories and over an ever-expanding range of activities. The outward drive threatens international peace; the inward drive jeopardizes individual liberty. The two in combination exercise a subtly corrupting influence on those who wield political power.

Majority rule. Since the state must have unlimited power to coerce, the prospects for liberty may well depend, first, upon the method of deciding what the state may legitimately undertake, and, second, upon the method of selecting and controlling those who exercise its awesome powers. The democratic way is through the process used in discovering the will of large voluntary groups—discussion and voting. This way is educational and gets results, two very great merits. Its greatest defect has already been mentioned: it cannot satisfy the wishes of the minority.

Democracy has been defined as the art of compromise and majority rule.[5] It might also be defined as government by discussion.[6] The willingness to discuss, to debate, and to delay action until an acceptable compromise is found presupposes patience and tolerance. These virtues are difficult to practice because few members of the minority can effectively exercise the right of withdrawal that makes majority rule work so satisfactorily in the case of voluntary groups.

The willingness to compromise is further weakened whenever a people come to believe that the will of the majority is the *only test* for determining what the state should and should not do. Compromise all but disappears when the majority come to believe that what they want is morally right. All too often majorities confuse their will with the will of God.

When this happens the way is open to a far more oppressive tyranny than that of any monarch claiming to rule by divine right. In the Age of Enlightenment the French people sent to the guillotine a weak and amiable king who genuinely believed that he lacked the power to correct ancient abuses. In his place they enthroned the Goddess of Reason in the form of a popularly elected assembly which could make and unmake law by simple majority vote. They thus ushered in a concept of sovereignty which scholars of an earlier age had regarded with abhorrence. And with good reason. Within a few years the Republic which was to bring liberty, equality, and fraternity to all the civilized world had "made terror part of the governmental process and ideology an instrument of war."[7]

· THE NEED FOR A CONSENSUS ·

More than patience and tolerance are needed if majority rule is to work. There must be large areas of agreement. A substantial majority must accept certain values without question and as a matter of course. Fortunately there are many issues on which the majority in the West are in reasonable agreement. Most of us want freedom of speech, freedom of assembly, and freedom of the press. We cherish religious freedom. We want the right to compete for public office without regard to race, color, or creed. We want to choose those who make and enforce the laws under which we live. We want some say in the way our children are educated. We prize the right to choose our jobs and, within very wide limits, to use our earnings as we see fit. Most of us want the right to save and to provide for our children after our deaths.

These are precisely the things which have already been fairly well realized in the countries of the West, and can be more completely realized without radical changes in existing institutional arrangements. Does it follow that most of us endorse the system of free enterprise which has been part of these arrangements? It is not at all certain. Many, perhaps a majority, like the eminent Italian philosopher Benedetto Croce,[8] see no causal connection between our ample freedoms, our tremendous wealth, and the methods by which the hopes and the ambitions of millions of persons have been harnessed and made to serve our varied needs with a minimum of coercion. And seeing no causal relationship, it is not surprising that we ask ourselves whether this voluntary system, despite its admitted productivity, could not be made to distribute its rewards more equally.

The next step is easy. If the will of the majority is the only valid test of what is right, and if the majority regard the present distribution of wealth as unjust, then surely it is the duty of the state to redress injustice by taking from those who have too much and giving to those who do not have enough.[9]

Democracy and Equality

The free enterprise system can take in its stride a very considerable political redistribution of wealth and income.[10] But there are limits. Can a democratic people stay within these limits? Doubts have been repeatedly expressed. De Tocqueville's warning has a prophetic ring:

> Democratic people have a natural taste for liberty; left to themselves they will seek it, cherish it, and be sad if it is taken from them. But their passion for equality is ardent, insatiable, eternal, and invincible. They want equality in freedom, but if they cannot have that, they still want equality in slavery. . . .[11]

> [Their] hatred of privilege increases as privileges become rarer and less important, the flame of democratic passion apparently blazing the brighter the less fuel there is to feed it. . . . When conditions are unequal, no inequality, however great, offends the eye. But amid general uniformity, the slightest dissimilarity seems shocking, and the completer the uniformity, the more unbearable it seems. It is therefore natural that love of equality should grow constantly with equality itself; everything done to satisfy it makes it grow.[12]

This latter passage is followed immediately by another which has particular relevance to a country of continental size like the United States.

> This ever-fiercer fire of endless hatred felt by democracies against the slightest privileges singularly favors the gradual concentration of all political rights in those hands which alone represent the state. . . . Every central power which follows its natural instincts loves equality and favors it. For equality singularly facilitates, extends, and secures its influence. One can also assert that every central government worships uniformity; uniformity saves it the trouble of inquiring into infinite details, which would be necessary if the rules were made to suit men instead of subjecting all men indiscriminately to the same rule.[13]

Warnings could be multiplied. To Woodrow Wilson the history of liberty was the history of the limitation of governmental power. "When I resist, therefore, the concentration of power, I am resisting the processes of death, because the concentration of power always precedes the destruction of liberty."[14] The late Justice Louis Brandeis urged us to be "most on our guard . . . when the government's purposes are beneficent. Men born to freedom are naturally alert to repel invasion of their liberty by evil-minded rulers. The greatest danger to liberty lurks in insidious encroachments by men of zeal, well meaning, but without understanding."[15] And this from Mahatma Gandhi:

> I look upon an increase in the power of the State with the greatest fear, because, while apparently doing good by minimizing exploitation, it does the greatest harm to mankind by destroying individuality which is the root of all progress. . . . In the ideal State, therefore, there is no political power because there is no State. But the ideal is never fully realized. Hence the classical statement of Thoreau that that government is best which governs least.[16]

Clearly, democracy has a strong bias against large social and material inequalities. Yet such inequalities have characterized all social systems. Societies based on private property and free enterprise, although they have generated fewer inequalities than any others, are no exception. Does this mean that there can be no lasting place for free enterprise in democratic societies? If this is so, and if Professor Wilhelm Roepke is correct[17] in asserting that political and spiritual liberty are impossible without economic liberty, then liberty itself turns out to be a mirage.

We are thus back to the dilemma posed at the outset. Without the state there can be neither liberty nor order. With the state we can have order without liberty. To have both we must find ways to control the omnipotence of the state. In the chapters that follow it will be argued that in a country of any size the best way—perhaps the only way—is through majority rule, not as the French of the Enlightenment conceived it, but as a group of colonials gathered at Philadelphia 180 years ago understood it: majority rule checked and controlled by a principle of equity that goes back to the Greeks—*the rule of law*—and by an entirely new political principle invented by these Colonials—*federalism.*

3

The State
and the Rule
of Law

IN ALL SOCIETIES the individual has some personal freedom, some area within which he may do as he pleases. The boundaries of this area of freedom are set by a combination of custom, command, and contract. Historically, progress toward freedom, as it is understood in the West, has been from custom through law to contract.

· COMMAND VERSUS CUSTOM ·

In primitive societies custom largely sets the boundaries and usually sets them very narrowly. But so long as individuals regard these boundaries as natural they do not feel restricted. The folkways are their ways.

As societies evolve the role of custom declines while that of authority or command, now in the guise of law, grows. Many of these commands, codifications of customary ways, will not be felt as restraints on freedom. Yet there are significant differences between laws and customs.

Customs, having the approval of the majority, promote social harmony. They do not have to be enforced by command. They can be broken by anyone who has the courage of his convictions. If the results prove beneficial, the new ways gradually become part of the customary ways. Custom can be terribly tyrannical, yet it possesses a flexibility law lacks.

Law is rigid. It cannot make fine distinctions. It either permits or forbids. The state is in jeopardy when its laws are openly flouted, as they invariably are when they cease to express the prevailing sense of justice. The Romans pictured Law as a blindfolded goddess. Rich and poor were supposed to stand equal before her, to obey her or to take the consequences in the form of known penalties. The goddess did not ask who stood at the bar before rendering judgment. This is, of course, an ideal which has never been fully realized, but a society is in a bad way when the ideal itself is rejected.

· LAW VERSUS THE RULE OF LAW ·

The term "rule of law" is peculiar to the English-speaking peoples.[1] It implies the existence of some limit, some higher principle, which Authority is bound to respect. German political theorists speak of the *Rechtsstaat*, or the state in which right prevails. French scholars use such terms as "the principle of legality." Wherever men have enjoyed freedom they have found some way of asserting the existence of a higher principle binding on rulers and ruled alike. Wherever those wielding power have failed to respect this higher principle, their statutes were commands, not laws; their orders rested on fear, not justice.

The Greek Contribution

The Greeks were the first people to make the distinction between a simple statute, or "ordinary" law, and "ideal" or "natural" law. By "natural" they meant no more than that a command must seem to a substantial majority of the people to be right and proper. It did not have to be written. It was binding because it expressed a moral consensus. In this respect law and custom were alike. But of one thing the Athenians, and the Greeks generally, were sure: The passing whims of majorities would seldom represent law in the "ideal" sense. "There can be no freedom," wrote Aristotle in *The Politics*, "where everything is determined by majority vote and not by law."[2]

Dean B. Roscoe Pound of the Harvard Law School regarded the discovery of the distinction between command and law the greatest and most permanent contribution of Greek thought to the philosophy of law.[3] D. V. Cowen, another eminent scholar, who has seen the spirit of the law increasingly flouted in his own country (South Africa), claims that it was respect for this distinction which "entitled the Greeks in their glory to say with justifiable pride that they enjoyed 'freedom under the law.'"[4] The Greek historian Herodotus put the idea of this higher law into the mouth of an exiled Spartan king at the Persian court: "Although the Greeks are free men, they are not free in every respect. Law is the master they own, and this master they fear more than any of thy subjects fear thee."[5] It is a central theme in Pericles' celebrated funeral oration:

> Our laws secure equal justice for all in their private disputes
> . . . [and] in our public acts we keep strictly within the control of the law. We acknowledge the restraint of reverence; we
> are obedient to whosoever is set in authority and to the laws,
> more especially to those which offer protection to the op-

pressed, and to those unwritten ordinances whose transgression brings admitted shame.[6]

Euripides defined a slave as "one who cannot speak his thoughts."[7]

And what wonders this new idea accomplished. In a period hardly longer than that which separates us from Colonial America, Athens made a contribution which, in the words of Edith Hamilton,

> so moulded the world of mind and spirit that our mind and spirit today are different. We think and feel differently because of what a little Greek town did during a century or two, twenty-four hundred years ago. What was then produced of art and thought has never been surpassed and very rarely equalled. And the stamp of it is on all the art and all the thought of the Western world. . . . A new civilization had arisen . . . unlike all that had gone before.[8]

The Greeks had discovered a great truth—that freedom is possible only where men are under law.

The Roman Contribution

Rome conquered Greece and in turn was conquered by the Greek concept of law. Cicero, like Cato before him, attributed the superiority of the Roman Constitution to all others to the fact that it "was based not upon the genius of one man, but of many; it was founded not in one generation, but in the long period of several centuries of men. . . . If it were possible to establish justice by the commands of the people, by the decrees of princes, by the adjudication of magistrates, then all that would be necessary in order to make robbery, adultery, or the falsification of wills right and just would be the vote of the multitude."[9]

Little use was made of what we call statute law. The rules for settling disputes among Roman citizens were "discovered" from a study of ancient practices. The great body of law was thus "immune from sudden and unpredictable change." Romans *knew* what they could and could not do, and hence could boast that they were free.[10]

In the course of time the ancient checks on power weakened and Romans again knew the meaning of tyranny. Yet it differed in one important respect from all the tyrannies which had gone before. Until the final collapse of the Empire in the East, the emperors, without exception, admitted that they were under law. An imperial edict issued in 429 A.D. expressed the prevailing view:

> . . . to acknowledge himself bound by the law is, for the sovereign, an utterance befitting the majesty of a ruler. For the truth is that our authority depends on the authority of the law. To submit our sovereignty to the laws is verily a greater thing than the Imperial Power.[11]

"Deep respect for the rules of law and their systematic observation," writes Professor J. B. Bury in his *History of the Later Roman Empire*. "characterized the Roman autocracy down to the fall of the Empire [in the East] in the fifteenth century, and was one of the conditions of its long duration. It was never an arbitrary despotism, and the masses looked up to the Emperor as the guardian of the laws which protected them against the oppression of nobles and officials."[12]

The Catholic Church and the Rule of Law

As Rome's secular power crumbled, anything deserving the name of civilization all but disappeared from Western Europe. Yet the concept of a higher law persisted within the Church and, in time, reappeared with a religious sanction. By the end of the thirteenth century the great principles of what came to be known as English Common Law were understood very much as they are today.

On these foundations a new order arose, built like those of Greece and Rome upon a collection of ancient practices. But now they were endowed with a supernatural sanction. To men of the Middle Ages it was self-evident that "the State cannot itself create or make law and as little abolish or violate law, because this would mean to abolish justice . . . a rebellion against God who alone creates law."[13] The ruler's task was to discover God's will. Those who held political power had to adapt themselves to the moral order; the moral order could not be required to adapt itself to them.[14] The monarchs-by-divine-right of the Middle Ages had less power than modern dictators, who invariably claim that they rule by the will of the people.

Law in the Age of Enlightenment

Medieval man was primarily concerned with gaining particular liberties—the right to do specific things. It took several hundred years before the modern concept of freedom emerged: "a condition in which all is permitted that is not prohibited by general rules."[15]

We owe this broader concept primarily to John Locke. In his *Second Treatise of Government* (1690)[16] he wrote,

> Freedom of men under government is to have a standing rule to live by, common to everyone of that society, and made by the legislative power erected in it; a liberty to follow my own will in all things where the rule prescribes not; and not to be subject to the inconstant, uncertain, unknown, arbitrary will of another man. (Sec. 22)

And Locke goes on,

> Whosoever has the legislative or supreme power of any commonwealth is bound to govern by established standing laws promulgated and known to the people, and not by extemporary decrees; by indifferent (i.e., by impartial) and upright judges,

who are to decide controversies by these laws and to apply the force of the community at home only in the execution of such laws. (Sec. 131)

If the citizen is to be free, the government official must be bound. Under a government of laws, as distinguished from a government of men, an individual acting in his private capacity may do *whatever* is not legally forbidden, whereas this same individual acting in his official capacity and with the power of the state behind him may do only that which is legally permitted. Otherwise the individual can never know in fact what he can do. "The executive," Locke emphasized, "should have no power but that of the law." (Sec. 151)

The men of the Enlightenment thought of the rule of law as a body of abstract rules defining the boundaries of the individual's *private sphere* and protecting him from coercion within this sphere. A major purpose of government was to protect such rights, and the proper method was through the definition and protection of property rights. To them it was self-evident *that there could be no human rights in the absence of property rights.*

Governmental orders, wherever possible, were to take the form of prohibitions, of "shall-nots," rather than directives, orders to do specific things. Whatever was not forbidden was to be permitted. This is very different from saying that all is forbidden that is not specifically permitted. It greatly increases the individual's range of choices. When his choices produced clearly harmful results, laws should be modified—either by changes in the interpretation of existing laws by "indifferent and upright judges," or by new statutes "made by the legislative power," and hence reflecting the judgment of the many, not of a single man. Here Locke, as a believer in government by consent, recognized the rightness and the merit of majority rule. But he coupled his endorsement with two important provisos. The first was that the members of the majority should know in advance that they would have to share the costs of the change with those, the minority, who would be hurt. This is the *principle of compensation*.[17] It leads majorities to be more considerate of minority interests and minority views. The second proviso was that changes should not be so frequent and so complex as to be incomprehensible.[18]

Men of the eighteenth century, having lived under arbitrary rule, recognized the high importance of *certainty*. To be *true law*, a measure had to apply to all and not merely to particular groups or persons, *unless* there was a relevant reason for treating them differently. It permitted children to be treated differently from adults, women differently from men. Further, it had to be certain and general, rather than specific and concrete, and applicable to future, not past, action. *Habeas corpus*, a safeguard against illegal imprisonment, and *due process*, or the right of a hearing and appeal to an independent judiciary, were regarded as essential protections of individual liberty, and hence as parts of the rule of law. For a statute to satisfy the stern tests of the rule it had to be known and so clearly stated that a court's decision on a complaint coming before it could be predicted with reasonable assurance once all the facts in the case were set forth.

The rule of law was concerned with *what the law should be*. That a statute had been legally enacted did not make it law in the ideal sense. Many so-called laws were nothing more than commands or orders, telling an individual *what he had to do*, leaving him no option. The purpose of *true law* was to tell him what he should not do, and what would be the consequence of disobedience. *True law* widened an individual's range of effective knowledge while still leaving him a wide range of choice. Men could not be free in a command society; they could be free in a society governed by the rule of law. Indeed, declared Locke, it was only in such a society that he could be free.

The Rule of Law in Today's World

Clearly, the rule of law is an aspiration. It expresses a belief that certain principles must be respected and certain procedures followed whenever lawmaking bodies make new laws or change old ones. Insofar as it is effective, it represents a limitation on all legislation, and hence on sovereignty itself. It cannot prevail unless it forms part of a moral tradition of the community, a common ideal, shared and unquestionably accepted by the majority. Ideally, then, the rule is a curb on the majority itself, and thus a denial of the modern view that whatever the majority wants is both right and desirable.[19]

Many legal scholars now challenge the above concept of the rule of law.[20] The accepted view in France, for example, and perhaps in Great Britain as well, is that the rule of law, or to use the French expression, "the principle of legality," constitutes a check on the Executive and on the administrative agencies to which the Executive or the Legislature may delegate power, not on the lawmaking authority itself. According to this interpretation, the only responsibility of an independent judiciary is to see that the Executive respects the spirit as well as the letter of all laws properly passed by a majority of the elected representatives of the people. This interpretation makes the rule of law nothing more than a legitimization of majority rule.

How is liberty likely to fare under this interpretation? It sanctioned two Napoleonic despotisms in France and paved the way for a Mussolini in Italy and a Hitler in Germany. Perhaps it will fare better in Anglo-Saxon countries. A glance at recent developments in England, however, is not encouraging. In wartime individual liberties have to be drastically restricted. But four years after the end of World War II—and what was true then is almost equally true today[21]—the list of things an Englishman might not do at all, or only with

explicit and tediously obtained permission, was still disquietingly long. According to an article in *Lloyd's Bank Review*
for August 1949,

> A man might not build himself a house, nor change his occu-
> pation, nor open, equip and operate a business, nor, if a
> farmer, rotate his crops, nor, if a shop-keeper, supply what his
> customers wanted, nor, if a professional man, import books
> essential to his work, nor travel abroad without more or less
> detailed official sanction; he could not correspond with his
> friends overseas without the risk of having his letters tampered
> with; he could not regulate the laying out of his income, since
> that was either directly determined by rationing and the pro-
> vision through tax on that income of communal services, or
> more subtly directed by the apparatus of special taxes and sub-
> sidy.

All these restrictions were enforced by departments of government which stood beyond the reach of the judiciary. This
situation led Professor G. W. Keeton, when he was Dean of
the Faculty of Law of the University of London, to ask whether
the rule of law and the sovereignty of Parliament had not become "polite and increasingly meaningless fictions."[22] His
question is the more significant because he was in general
sympathy with the objectives of the government.

This was in 1952. Two years later Professor C. J. Hamson,
another eminent legal scholar, expressed his concern at the
helplessness of the average Englishman in the face of arbitrary
executive power:

> There is . . . an increasingly important territory into which
> the writs of the High Court no longer effectively run . . . a
> domain which, in England, the Executive has made its own,
> in which its own will is paramount and unsubjected to any
> kind of judicial supervision. . . . The Administrative act can-
> not be inquired into. The decision emanates from the office or
> the department, with or without a reason adduced, as the
> official may choose. . . . Sometimes the act is unjust; and very

often it is either in appearance arbitrary or it is sanctioned by arbitrary power visibly held in reserve.

Then comes his disquieting conclusion:

The final essential arbitrariness of the *lawful* administrative act causes in England a resentment and an anger which, in my opinion, are dangerous to the body politic.[23]

The Rule of Law and the Welfare State

Until quite recently the courts of Great Britain (and of the United States) were concerned primarily with the rights of individuals and only secondarily with the workings of the national economy. The latter was left largely to the market forces with which we shall be concerned presently. The task of government was to provide a legal framework within which free enterprise could function. It was taken for granted that statutes should be subject to review and acts of administrative agencies halted by injunction if necessary, while the courts decided on the validity of complaints by individuals that their legitimate rights had been violated.[24]

Can this position be maintained in a society in which the electorate holds government responsible for the smooth functioning of the economy? Can the wheels of industry be stopped while the courts decide where justice lies in the disputes among individuals regarding the legality of governmental rulings? Must not the administrative agencies be given not only the power to issue appropriate rules, but also the power to hear and settle the disputes among individuals which are bound to result from their rulings?

Here is a crucial issue in the whole contemporary debate regarding the possible threat to freedom arising from comprehensive economic planning.[25] Such planning requires rigid priorities. Many attractive outlets for individual initiative have to be closed. Energies and resources have to be directed into a few defined channels. To do this by the shall-not type of regulation required by the rule of law would hopelessly complicate the law-making processes. No one could be sure that he was acting within the law. Planning laws must use ambiguous words like "fair," "equitable," "reasonable," "adequate," "just," etc., and a bureaucracy must then be given final authority to hear and settle complaints. The whole apparatus of production cannot be stopped while the courts weigh the rights of complainants against the necessities of the plan. Broad and sweeping discretion is essential to efficient planning.

The rule of law, whether it be interpreted as a check on the Executive and the administrative agencies only, or on the lawmakers as well, stands in the way of this kind of planning. But the rule of law, as an abstract principle, is not strong enough to resist the demands of popular majorities, particularly in societies in which most elected officials take it for granted that their task is to discover and carry out the will of the majority. The whole record of history shows that something more is needed. It will be argued in the next chapter that federalism may provide this extra something.

4

Federalism

TIME.HAS A WAY of changing the meaning of words. Liberalism and "the rule of law" do not mean to the young of today what they meant to an earlier generation. This is particularly true of the word "federalism." We shall use it as K. C. Wheare, a recognized authority on comparative government, uses it. A federation is a permanent political association in which a few precisely defined powers are assigned exclusively to a central government, a limited number are shared, and the rest are retained and exercised only by the member states.[1] The United States is the oldest and one of the very few genuinely federal associations. The separation of powers finds clear expression in the Tenth Amendment to the Constitution of the United States:

> The powers not delegated to the United States by the Constitution, nor prohibited by it to the States, are reserved to the States respectively, or to the people.

· THE FEDERAL PRINCIPLE ·

Dual citizenship. In a federation there is *dual citizenship.*
The central government and the member states derive their
mandates directly from the people; the authority of the government and the states is based on *written* documents or constitutions. These constitutions must be an expression of the
views of a substantial majority of the voters at the time of
adoption, and must be subject to alteration (amendment)
only by elaborate and time-consuming processes and again by
a vote of a substantial majority of all qualified voters, though
not necessarily a majority of the voters in every state. Disputes
regarding the consistency of statutes and executive acts with
the provisions of the Constitution must be subject to binding
arbitration by an independent judiciary, which is itself bound
by the Constitution.

The importance of permanence. If a federal system is to
work, its Constitution must be taken seriously. The French
and the American Republics both date from the last years of
the eighteenth century. The American Constitution stands
virtually intact. It has been amended only fifteen times in
over 175 years, if we count, as we should, the ten Bill of
Rights Amendments of 1789 as part of the original document. French Constitutions, on the other hand—19 in all
since the Revolution of 1789—"have been too precarious to
be stable, and too numerous to be either remembered or
respected."[2]

Fiscal autonomy. In a federal system the central government and the member states are separate but equal. Fiscal
independence is essential. If the central government depends
on grants from the member states, we have a league or
confederation, not a federation.[3] The United Nations organization is a league, not a federation. If the member states

depend on the central government for funds, we have in effect a unitary government, though elements of a federal past may linger on for some time.

Because it is more difficult for persons to escape its jurisdiction, the central government in a federation is a better money raiser than are the member states. Consequently, the life of a federation in the world of today is likely to be short unless ways can be found for transferring to the member states, without strings, and according to a formula written into the Constitution itself, a portion of the revenues raised by the central government.

States' rights. People will not voluntarily enter a federal system unless they know that what today is called "states' rights" will be scrupulously respected. In this age of rampant nationalism the peoples of the West would not surrender as many elements of sovereignty to a central government as did the Americans in 1787 unless they were satisfied that they could continue to manage their domestic affairs as they saw fit.

The importance of tolerance. In a federation majorities in the several states must reconcile themselves to the fact that majorities in the other states will again and again handle domestic affairs—matters expressly reserved to them in the compact of union—in ways they do not approve of. Local loyalties—what, at the turn of the century the philosopher Josiah Royce had called "wholesome parochialism"—must be respected if such a union is not to become, in his words, "an incomprehensible monster in whose presence the individual loses his rights, his self-consciousness, his dignity."[4] A half century later, the French political philosopher Bertrand de Jouvenal echoed the same warning. "The big state is a bad thing in itself. It becomes all the more blind to individual realities as its size increases. It becomes more inhuman, more geometric, more automatic."[5] He stressed a point we shall come back to in our discussion of the efforts of the central government in this country to promote a more just pattern of wages—the tendency to treat "unequal cases in a uniform way." This tendency is particularly dangerous in a country of continental size. The verdict of history may well be that such a country will be governed either as a federation or as an autocracy.[6]

Federalism and the rule of law. A federation can include kingdoms as well as republics, democracies as well as aristocracies. The essential condition for membership is acceptance of the rule of law. A socialist state, or indeed a state in which the government undertakes to plan economic life in detail, cannot enter a federation because, as we have seen, it cannot be fettered by the rule of law.[7] It cannot have its plans altered in response to every passing whim of the electorate. It cannot allow goods and people to move freely into and out of its territories. Comprehensive planning requires the concentration, not the diffusion, of political power. An advocate of capitalism can logically advocate federalism; a socialist cannot. If the people of the United States want socialism, they must scrap the last vestiges of federalism. If the peoples of the West want a wider union and socialism, they must be prepared to give up their national identities. If they want a wider union while yet keeping their national identities, they must give up the dream of socialism.

· THE AMERICAN FEDERAL SYSTEM ·

The original United States of America was a league or confederation. It had been strong enough to fight to a successful conclusion a war against the most powerful country in the world, but it was not strong enough to prevent quarrels among the confederates once the war was over. Inflation was rampant. Trade rivalries and boundary disputes had provoked armed clashes. The central government was bankrupt. There was a very real possibility that the British Crown would regain most of its lost colonies before the century closed. The discovery of the federal principle was almost literally the child of necessity. What the Founding Fathers sought and invented was a new form of government which could at one and the same time satisfy the people's love of liberty, protect their rights as citizens, quiet their suspicions of distant and centralized government, and still give to that central government enough power to assure domestic order and protection against foreign aggression.

The main features of the American federal system are well known. It is a two-level association with a separation of the legislative and executive powers at both the central and the state levels and the subordination of both to an independent judiciary, whose decisions, however, are to be based on written constitutions. Since these constitutions are the products of elaborate discussion, must be ratified by substantial majorities, and can only be changed by equally elaborate and time-consuming procedures, they play the role in the American federal system of that higher law which the ancients found in the wisdom of their ancestors and medieval man believed to be reflected in the will of God. State constitutions must be consistent with the Constitution of the United States. The federal principle rejects the thesis that whatever the majority of the people's elected representatives favor is right and hence is law. State constitutions represent a higher law. The Constitution of the United States is the highest law.

The central government was given the exclusive power to regulate commerce and population movements among the states and with foreign countries, to levy import duties, to coin

money and regulate its value, to declare war, and to raise
and support military forces. The states could no longer control
their monetary systems. Currency devaluations, exchange controls, and physical limitations on imports (quotas) could no
longer be used to protect their domestic markets or to give
them a price advantage in foreign markets. They were thus
committed to the traditional Liberal ideal—complete and un-
conditional free trade. Except for its exclusive power to levy
import duties, the central government shared the taxing
power with the states, subject, however, to a uniformity requirement that in the end weakened federalism by making it
difficult for either the central government or the state governments to provide services required by an increasingly urbanized and industrialized society.

Distrust of Government

So great was the distrust of government, and especially of
distant government, that those elected under the new Constitution passed at their very first session ten amendments
designed to limit the powers of government at all levels. These
amendments are known as the Bill of Rights. The First denied
to the central government the power to establish a state re-
ligion, or to abridge freedom of speech, freedom of the press,
or the right of peaceful assembly for religious or other purposes. The Fifth Amendment denied to both levels of government the power to deprive a person "of life, liberty, or property
without due process of law" or to take private property "for
public use without just compensation." The prevailing fear of
government came out with particular clarity in the Ninth and
Tenth Amendments. The Ninth stated that the enumeration in
the Constitution of certain rights was not to be construed as
denying or disparaging others retained by the people. The
Tenth Amendment, as already noted, reserved to the states,

or to the people, powers not expressly delegated to the central government.

While the Founding Fathers shared the prevailing distrust of government power, they had no intention of creating a pure democracy such as the French were shortly to adopt. They recognized that the will of the majority not only would but should prevail in the long run. What they wanted were delaying tactics which would reconcile majority rule with the need for security, order, and liberty. They discovered that all three objectives could be realized (a) by so splitting sovereignty that no governmental unit acting alone could threaten freedom, (b) by putting the new arrangement into a written covenant which could not be easily amended, and hence would bind succeeding generations, and (c) by providing for the compulsory settlement of disputes by an independent judiciary. But unlike Locke's "indifferent and upright judges," these men were to be bound by their oaths of office to find the grounds for their decisions within the Constitution.

What the authors of the Constitution sought, in brief, was to realize the Greek ideal of "freedom under the law." Through an elaborate system of checks and balances they tried to establish a Binding Rule (the Constitution) for the making of rules (ordinary laws). It was their hope that in the course of time this Rule would come to command such veneration that lawmakers would dare resist the passing will of the majority in moments of crisis, "when," to quote James Madison, "the people, stimulated by some irregular passion, or some illicit advantage or misled by the artful misrepresentations of interested men, will call for measures which they themselves will afterwards be the most ready to lament and condemn."[8]

The French have had troubles with their constitutions because they insist on making democracy a supreme end rather than an ultimate sanction. The American Constitution was written by democrats who feared democracy. The principle of one-man one-vote, an expression *par excellence* of the new democratic principle, was not to apply to the upper house in the new government. The votes of the two senators from Rhode Island were to count for as much as those of the two from New York. Nor was the principle reflected in the presidential veto, which could only be overruled by a two-thirds vote of both houses of the Congress, nor in the Supreme Court, where seven men (now nine), appointed to office for life with salaries which could be increased but not decreased (other than by inflation), could by a simple majority vote override the will of all the people insofar as it came before them in the form of a statute against which a complaint of unconstitutionality had been raised. The statute might have had the approval of Congress, of the President, of all the state governors, of all members of state legislatures and all members of state courts and lower federal courts.

It is, of course, most improbable that a majority in the Supreme Court of the United States would ever hold unconstitutional a law with such backing. But in recent years and with increasing frequency the Court has voided old laws which had such long acceptance as to have acquired that certainty which Roman jurists had rightly regarded as a vital part of the rule of law.[9] The Dred Scott decision (1857), in outlawing a compromise of thirty-six years standing (the Missouri Compromise prohibiting the extension of slavery into the territories north of the Mason-Dixon line) and regarded at the time as hardly less sacred than the Constitution itself, destroyed the chance of solving the slavery issue peacefully and by the method required by the rule of law—emancipation with compensation. This was the method successfully followed by Great Britain and the countries of Central and South America during the first half of the nineteenth century. In 1954 the Court reversed the "separate but equal" doctrine laid down in *Plessy v. Ferguson* but inexcusably ignored for sixty years by the Congress, the Executive, and the Court itself. Then with its *Brown v. Topeka Board of Education* decision it went to the other extreme. By finding segregation inequitable *per se* it precipitated a crisis which may prove as serious as that produced by Chief Justice Taney's *obiter dictum* in the Dred Scot case. The Court's one-man, one-vote decision of 1962 (*Baker et al v. Carr*) disregarded a practice that dated back to the first days of the federal experiment. Its 1967 interpretation of the 14th Amendment limits the right of an individual to sell his property to the person of his choice far more narrowly than the Congress regarded as expedient. The majority of the judges in the Court, as presently constituted, no longer feel obliged to seek the grounds for their decisions in ancient precedents, or within the Constitution. They find them within their own consciences. This has introduced that uncertainty against which Hamilton and Madison had warned in a celebrated passage in the *Federalist Papers* (*No. 62*):

> The internal effects of a mutable policy are still more calamitous [than the external effects]. It poisons the blessings of liberty itself. It will be of little avail to the people that the laws are made by men of their own choice, if the laws be so voluminous that they cannot be read; or so incoherent that they cannot be understood; if they be repealed or revised before they are promulgated; or undergo such incessant changes that no man, who knows what the law is today, can guess what it will be tomorrow. Law is defined as a rule of action, but how can that be a rule which is little known and less fixed.

These developments suggest that both federalism, as the Founding Fathers understood it, and the pure democracy of the French Revolution may be in jeopardy in the United States. We appear to be approaching Plato's ideal Republic where philosophers are to rule.

· THE DECLINE OF FEDERALISM ·

The loss of faith in federalism is relatively recent. Why?
There is no simple explanation. One important reason, I am
persuaded, was the failure to provide in the Constitution itself
arrangements which would assure to both the state governments and the central government the revenues needed for
the discharge of the functions assigned to them.

The Taxing Power

The Constitution denied to the central government the
power to levy taxes on exports and required that direct taxes
had to be apportioned, i.e., distributed among the states in
proportion to their populations. A direct tax was understood
to mean a tax on land, buildings, cattle, slaves, and other
tangible evidences of wealth.[10] In effect, therefore, the only
direct tax the central government could levy was a flat and
uniform poll tax, a tax which would have been both unproduc-
tive and unpopular. The Congress was thus forced to rely almost entirely on revenues derived from the sale of the public
domain and on customs duties and internal excises. The latter
are indirect taxes which take relatively more of a poor man's
income than of a rich man's. In the language of economics
they are *regressive*. A welfare program dependent on such
taxes lacks political appeal. Few votes are to be had by promising services which will cost the beneficiaries more than they
would have to pay for them in the open market—unless they
can be persuaded that someone else is paying. For this a
graduated income tax is highly useful, at least in the beginning.[11]

The Constitution denied to the states the power to levy
taxes on goods entering or leaving their territories. They re-

tained all other powers, and thus could, from a strictly legal point of view, distribute the burden of taxation in any way local majorities saw fit. In fact the states have to treat persons of wealth gently, lest they leave, taking their possessions with them. Nor can a wealthy minority exploit the majority by forcing them to buy from high-priced local producers or to work for less than producers in other states will pay. Federalism enforces competition, and competition in turn protects people as producers and consumers.

For a century and a quarter these two limitations, one on the central government, the other on the state governments, made impossible any radical redistribution of incomes from the well-to-do to the poor. Whether the Founding Fathers realized it or not, they had imposed upon the country what we called earlier (p. 8) the free enterprise system. Here it suffices to note that one result of their labors was a revenue system which was highly regressive and hence entirely reprehensible from the modern liberal point of view. It was, however, very conducive to risk taking, saving, investing, and growth in a country on the threshold of development and blessed with an abundance of natural resources. Furthermore its main beneficiaries would be the poor, not least Europe's "huddled masses, yearning to be free," who would come by the tens of thousands annually to share in and contribute to a comfort and a dignity undreamed of in their former homes.

The Spending Power

In the kind of world we live in today, the central government in a federation must have unlimited taxing power if it is to meet its major responsibility, national defense. This introduces a complication. The unlimited taxing power essential to survival in time of war can become a threat to a federation in time of peace, if it produces more money than is needed for the effective discharge of the limited functions for which federations are created. If it does, plausible reasons will be found for entering fields reserved to the states.

The threat was repeatedly pointed out in the early days of the Republic. John Adams and Thomas Jefferson held that the central government could spend *only* for the purposes clearly "enumerated" in the Constitution. Monroe, Jackson, Van Buren, and Tyler were willing to stretch the Constitution to cover expenditures for clearly national purposes, but they consistently vetoed bills for internal improvements involving only local benefits as "a subversion of the federal principle." Presidents Polk, Pierce, and Buchanan reverted to the earlier and stricter interpretations that John Adams had observed and Thomas Jefferson had preached. Franklin Pierce's May 3, 1854 veto of a bill to authorize a "grant of public lands to the several States for the benefit of indigent persons" anticipated by thirty-four years another and probably the last effort of a President to keep the central government out of the welfare field. "I cannot find any authority in the Constitution," Pierce wrote, "for making the Federal Government the great almoner of public charity throughout the United States." To do so would be "subversive of the whole theory upon which the union of these States is founded."[12]

The temptation to "subvert the federal principle," to employ the term so frequently used during this period, was present from the very beginning because of the decision made by the first Congress, to use tariffs for protective purposes. For many years customs duties produced substantial surpluses. These surpluses were used for the internal improvements, to which many of the Presidents objected, as well as for the reduction of the debts inherited from the Revolution, the Louisiana Purchase, and the War of 1812. Some of the spending was wise and entirely constitutional, but some was not. In his farewell address (1837), Andrew Jackson noted the subtly corrupting influence of protectionism and surpluses:

> In order to fasten upon the people this unjust and unequal system of taxation, extravagant schemes of internal improvement are got up in various quarters to squander the money and to purchase support. . . . The corporations and the wealthy individuals who are engaged in large manufacturing establishments, desire a high tariff to increase their gains. Designing politicians will support it to conciliate their favor, and to obtain the means for profuse expenditure, for the purpose of purchasing influence in other quarters. It is from within, among ourselves—from cupidity, from corruption, from disappointed ambition, and inordinate thirst for power—that factions will be formed and liberty endangered.

This expression of concern for the traditional virtues may come as a surprise to those who think of Andrew Jackson as "the father of the spoils system." Actually there was nothing inconsistent in his position on these two issues. He was convinced that if democracy was to survive power had to be limited, be it public or private. He also believed that the essential functions of government were few and simple and quite capable of being handled by honest men of ordinary intelligence. As a politician he realized that many of those who worked to get a man elected to office had to be rewarded. Unless jobs could be vacated at each new election, politicians would be under constant pressure to expand the functions of government to provide places for those active in the latest election. This pressure to expand the role of government seemed to him to threaten the general welfare even more than the wholesale turnover of personnel following elections.

Beginning with the Compromise Tariff of 1833, a slow movement toward free trade started. On the eve of the Civil War the country had something approaching the tariff-for-revenue-only system held by many to be the only type of tariff consistent with the federal principle. Unfortunately the new political party which was to end slavery was also the party of high protection. Consequently the federal system, as it emerged from the Civil War, was again confronted with the same subtly corrupting force against which Andrew Jackson had warned. Either the tariffs which produced surpluses had to be reduced, or the surpluses had to be spent. And again the Congress chose to spend.

Much of the spending was wasteful and of doubtful constitutionality. The phrase "pork-barrel legislation" dates from this period. From helping projects (post offices, harbor improvements, etc.) in politically sensitive communities, it was but a step to helping needy people in these same communities. The people's money was being used not only to keep inefficient industries alive, but also to buy the elections which perpetuated the system.

Grover Cleveland, the first post-Civil War Democratic President, appreciated the threat to federalism and like Andrew Jackson 50 years earlier protested vigorously but in vain. No President of recent years would dare veto a money grant to a state hit by a sudden natural disaster for the reason Cleveland offered: "lest the limited mission of the central government be forgotten, . . . that though the people should support the government, the government should not support the people."

This sounds heartless. It should be remembered, however, that the disaster had hit only one part of a large state and that the government of that state could have sold bonds in the open market and come to the aid of the stricken people had the majority of the voters been sufficiently concerned.

The Sixteenth Amendment

The foundations of federalism really began to crumble when the Sixteenth Amendment gave the central government the power to levy a direct and graduated tax on personal incomes without any restrictions as to how high the rates on the wealthy few might be pushed and on how many might be entirely exempted. The central government was at long last in a position to finance a full-fledged welfare program.

During the four years the Amendment was under consideration, 1909–1913, the annual expenditures of the central government never passed the billion-dollar mark. Many of those who would be liable to the new tax favored it as an offset to the inevitably regressive customs duties and excises on which the central government depended.

Few recognized how enormously popular spending by the central government could become with a public that could be easily persuaded that someone else would pay the bill for the many things they wanted, how easy it would be politically to push rates up in emergencies, and finally, how difficult it would be to get them down after an emergency had passed. It took twenty years to get the top rate down to 70 percent from a confiscatory 91 percent, even though the rates above 50 percent yield very little revenue. This does not mean that such rates are harmless.[13] On the contrary, they protect well-established businesses by making it difficult for newcomers to accumulate the capital needed for expansion, they retard growth, invite evasion and corruption, and, perhaps most serious of all, encourage extravagance by making the majority believe that they can safely vote new services for themselves, because a wealthy minority will pay the bill.

I do not want to be misunderstood. I favored the Sixteenth Amendment when it was under discussion and I still believe that in a world in which peace is only a distant dream the central government in a federation must have the power to levy such a tax. I am further persuaded, as will be argued presently,[14] that a politically acceptable amendment could prevent the abuses noted above.

· THE FUTURE OF FEDERALISM ·

Federalism at present is little more than a word, a theme for Fourth of July orations. Few candidates for public office venture to scoff at it publicly, no matter how flagrantly they violate its restraints once safely elected. In 1930, speaking over the radio in the early days of the Great Depression, Franklin D. Roosevelt, at the time governor of New York, described the American Constitution "as the most marvellously elastic compilation of rules ever written," and warned that any attempt by a national administration "to make all the laws for the whole nation . . . would inevitably result, at some future time, in the dissolution of the union itself."[15] In 1952, the late Adlai E. Stevenson, during his campaign for the presidency, urged that the central government "be left unencumbered in the discharge of its monstrous duties by a lot of other jobs it need not do. The states and local governments," he declared, "are the dikes we can build more strongly against the flood waters sweeping toward the District of Columbia."[16] In 1962, Nelson Rockefeller, another aspirant for the presidency, in a lecture given at Harvard University, after the usual obeisance to federalism as not only necessary to the defense of liberty at home but perhaps the only means by which liberty and order could be maintained in the world which yet stood outside the communist orbit, argued for a more generous use of grants-in-aid as the only way of saving it in the United States.[17] At the time he spoke grants from the central government to the state and local governments stood at less than $8 billion. Five years later they were approaching the $15 billion mark and the incumbent president was urging still larger transfers of income in the name of "creative federalism."

Some 70 percent of the central government's spending for domestic purposes now passes through the hands of state governments and their local subdivisions under close to 500 separate authorizations. It is difficult to turn out of office an administration that controls this amount of spending. A growing number of competent and impartial observers are recommending the substitution of a few consolidated grants with a minimum of strings attached as the remedy.[18]

The present system is a product of the Great Depression of the 1930s. In a single generation it has transformed the United States into something very close to the unitary republic the Founding Fathers feared, one in which the will of a simple nationwide majority could prevail. The states and their subdivisions have become so dependent on Washington that they are accepting programs poorly suited to their special needs and are administering them with little regard to efficiency and economy.[19] The subtle kind of corruption which Andrew Jackson and Grover Cleveland feared has come to be taken for granted. Congressmen frankly seek office by promising to get more out of Washington than their opponents. We appear to be killing federalism with the very benevolence which Justice Brandeis feared,[20] and which De Tocqueville referred to as that "tutelary power" which seeks to keep people in perpetual childhood, working for their happiness but wanting always to be "the sole agent and judge thereof."[21]

If federalism cannot survive this governmental benevolence, will capitalism be any more successful? Before trying to answer this question, we need to understand what capitalism is, how it works, and what the state should do and should refrain from doing if the majority of us really wish to preserve it.

5

The Way of the Market

THIS CHAPTER PRESENTS a highly simplified picture of the free enterprise system. It is a "model." Its purpose is to bring out a) the enormous productivity of the system, b) its egalitarian bias, and c) its compatibility both with the rule of law and federalism. The state plays a very limited role in this model, providing only those absolutely essential services which cannot be supplied at all by individuals or voluntary groups: the maintenance of internal order, protection against violence from without, and the enforcement of the innumerable agreements (contracts) upon which the performance of the system depends. A later chapter recognizes other important tasks the state must perform if a free enterprise system is to realize all its potential.

50

· THE CAPITALISTIC MODEL ·

A society, however it is organized, has to find answers to a number of critical questions: What shall be produced? How much? Where and by whom? How shall the output be divided? According to need? According to what each individual contributes? How much shall be set aside for the needs of the future?

In societies relying largely on individual initiative, the answers are derived from a set of signals which economists call *prices*. These prices appear whenever and wherever men are allowed to *specialize and trade* with one another on terms freely arrived at. Competition forces them to obey the signals. This is *the way of the market*. The alternatives are *custom* and *command*, both *ways of authority*.

In all societies there is an admixture of the two ways. Yet there is a significant difference. If government accepts the prices fixed in free markets, if it charges users of public services all the costs involved wherever this is technically possible, and finally, if it permits individuals and private groups to compete with it, then the way of the market prevails. What is decisive is not the size of the public sector but the location of the authority to make the critical decisions. Where this authority is diffused and disciplined by competition, the way of the market prevails; where it is concentrated and determined by the political processes, the way of authority prevails.

The Market Process

The term "market" is also used to describe the processes by which exchanges among specialists are effected. An exchange occurs after an agreement has been reached. Since the exchange is voluntary it can be taken for granted that all the parties to the transaction gain. The exchange may involve a "good" or a "service," something already on hand or something to be produced and delivered at a later date. Buyers and sellers may be few or many, depending on the size of the market. Within a single market all units of a given kind of good or service change hands on identical terms. Prices in local markets are influenced, of course, by conditions in neighboring markets. They cannot differ by more than transportation and other costs connected with moving goods from one market to another. Where these costs are insignificant, local markets tend to merge into regional, national, or even worldwide markets. Cheap transportation and rapid communication through the telephone, telegraph, and radio and television have enormously widened markets, increased the number of buyers and sellers, and made possible the mass production of many goods which in the past were the luxuries of a privileged few.

The market as a coordinator. In a market economy *the firm* is the coordinating agent—it may be a carpentry shop, a corner drugstore, or a giant concern employing thousands of people; it may be a single proprietor, a partnership, a corporation, or a cooperative. It brings together workers (labor) and physical resources (capital) and puts them to work making what people want, or what they can be persuaded to want. But before a firm can produce anything it must get workers and owners of physical resources to cooperate with it rather than with another firm. How does it do this? How does it decide what to produce, where and how to produce, and how to divide the output among all those involved? The answer again is: prices. They provide both signals and incentives.

The market as a rewarder. Some people prefer to go into business for themselves. They own the firms. They are their own bosses. They take the risks. They can never know in advance whether, at year's end, they will have made or lost money. For every risk taker there are a hundred who prefer to be job takers, to allow others to hire their services and use their physical resources—their property—on terms agreed upon in advance and payable regardless of the outcome.

Since risk takers can only guess what they will eventually get, they naturally offer the nonrisk takers, the workers and property owners, *as little as possible*, just enough to get all the resources they believe they can profitably use. And resource owners try to get *as much as possible*.

These groups meet in three types of markets: labor markets, real estate markets, and capital markets. If these markets are reasonably well organized, all who wish to hire out their services or to sell or rent their physical resources find takers, provided they do not ask more than the risk takers can afford to pay. The markets are said to be *cleared*. In the labor market *wages* emerge; in the real estate market, *rents*; in the capital market, *interest*. These are the prices the owners of the firms pay to workers and to those who supply land and capital. To the risk takers, they are costs; to the workers and the resource owners (the capitalists), they are income. Firms cannot afford to pay more, and workers and capitalists do not have to take less.

The market system is a profit-and-loss system. It rewards risk taking and penalizes waste. Since risk takers are congenitally optimistic—otherwise they would not be in business for themselves—many offer too much and hence make losses. They would have done better as job takers and interest and rent receivers. It is the hope of profits, much more than profits themselves, which keeps the system going and makes it efficient.

The Role of Profits

National income accounting exaggerates the profit com-
ponent. To find out whether risk takers as a group are making
any *net* profits, four deductions must be made from their
gross profits: (1) interest on the capital they put into their
own businesses; (2) the salaries they could have made working for others; (3) the direct taxes levied on the successful
risk takers; and (4) the losses of the unsuccessful ones. Because, to repeat, risk takers are optimists, overconfident of
their own capacities, and because they want to be their own
bosses, society gets the services of this small but very important group on very favorable terms. The incomes of the
successful ones, plus the returns going to them and to all
other property owners as interest and rents, amount to less
than 20 percent of the national income. Workers with hand
and brain get more than 80 percent, since a considerable
part of the so-called profits of professional people and individual proprietors are in reality wages.

Profits and losses largely cancel themselves out. Nonetheless, both play an enormously important role, perhaps the
most important one in the whole system. Profits tell businessmen that they should expand; losses tell them that they must
either improve their operations or quit and release resources
to firms which can make better use of them.

Consumer Sovereignty

Profits are proof that consumers are being well served;
losses that they are either not getting what they want, or that
the job is being done badly. Changes in profits cause changes
in the rewards firms pay to the nonrisk takers. But all of these
people, risk takers and nonrisk takers, are consumers. As their
incomes change, some rising, some falling, their spending

patterns change and again all the prices in the system change. The consumer calls the tune. He is the king, exacting and frequently capricious. He expects his servants to obey his every command. He rewards extravagantly those who bring to him strange delicacies and contrive new experiences, and banishes those who bore him. Yet his power is not absolute. He too is subject to a higher authority. He has to find someone who will hire him and pay him for the use of his resources. The consumer issues orders, but he also has to obey orders. No less than the business firms, he is subject to the market and its processes.

Political versus Market Decision Making

In a market economy every income receiver is a voter. His dollars are his ballots. He votes every day, every hour, in a dozen stores, not just every two or four years in the privacy of a polling booth. Firms, like political parties, compete for his dollars. But, unlike the latter, the firms neither know nor care whether the ballots they seek will be cast by Protestants or Catholics, by white men or black men, by cranks or by saints. They cannot allow their personal likes and dislikes to influence them. Competition forces them to serve majorities and minorities alike. They will provide a lady of fashion with a gown unlike any other in the world, but most of their energies are devoted to satisfying the wants of wage earners, because they cast most of the ballots. "The capitalistic achievement," as Joseph Schumpeter was fond of pointing out, "does not typically consist in providing more silk stockings for queens but in bringing them within the reach of factory girls in return for steadily decreasing amounts of work."[1]

On the other hand, firms do not and, if they are subject to competition, cannot cater to nonvoters, to those who have no incomes. They must be given ballots by relatives, friends, organized private charity, or by the state if their wishes are to be registered. Nor can firms, as we shall presently see, provide a number of services essential to civilized living. We cannot look to them for national defense, or law and order, or protection against contagious diseases because they have no way of withholding such services from those who want them but are unwilling to pay for them. These are collective services. If they are provided at all, they become available to all. Only the state can provide them because it has the power to tax. Old-fashioned Liberals recognize that there are many collective services which the state not only can but should provide. But they also recognize that when the state does so, it responds to a set of political signals. These, as we have seen, are quite different from those operating in the market, less precise but more compelling because they are backed by the coercive power of government. This means that many people have to pay for services they do not want. Sometimes they may even have to use the services against their wills. If a firm treated its customers as the state frequently treats its minorities, it would soon be out of business.

The inability of the state to respond to the wishes of minority groups is one reason why, quite aside from the threat to freedom that comes from the concentration of power, the Liberal looks first to the market for the solution of a problem, then to voluntary nonprofit associations, and only as a last resort to government, and then to the lowest possible level —to the town rather than the county, the county rather than the state, the state rather than the central government.

Competition

Competition is a form of rivalry which makes firms and resource owners offer more for less. A firm offers more for less when it improves quality or lowers prices. A worker offers more for less when he accepts a lower wage or works a bit harder. It is difficult to conceive of a surer road to abundance. Moreover the consumer can be king only in societies in which competition is effective.

How effective is competition in the United States today? If we accept the usual textbook definitions, with their emphasis on perfection and on the very short run, the answer is, "not very." But if we accept the rough and ready definition offered above and judge its performance over reasonable lengths of time, the market appears to be sufficiently competitive to justify the Liberal's confidence in it as an allocating and rewarding device.[2] The drive of self-interest which is built into the system explains its extraordinary productivity—a productivity Karl Marx, one of its bitterest critics, recognized in the celebrated passage in the *Communist Manifesto* to which reference was made earlier.[3]

The capitalistic performance has been even more impressive in the century since Marx delivered his fulsome eulogy. Yet today the system has been rejected by most of the people of the world. Why? In no small part, I am persuaded, because so many of the opinion makers of the world—Schumpeter's "intellectuals"[4]—have convinced themselves that a system which depends on the profit motive and competition cannot be ethical. Hence they have not even tried to understand how the system works, how efficient it is as a device for getting people to cooperate, and how effectively it disperses economic power and thus reduces to manageable proportions the tasks which the state and only the state can perform.

A special virture of the market is its capacity to minimize resentments. Whenever men look to the market for goods and services that it is technically able to provide, the vast majority come away at least partially satisfied and there is no clear target against which to direct their discontents. When they look to the state, many will get nothing, and will be deeply disappointed and fairly sure in their own minds where the blame lies. Their inevitable disappointments exacerbate discontents, cause them to be directed at persons, not circumstances, and weaken the willingness of large numbers to accept the verdict of the majority. The growing domestic violence in the United States and throughout the nontotalitarian world may well be due in part to the increasing tendency of people to demand of their governments services that the market and private philanthropic groups are quite capable of providing. Meantime, these governments, charged with tasks they are ill-fitted to perform, find it increasingly difficult to discharge their primary function—the maintenance of domestic order. They tend increasingly to meet violence with violence. Perhaps this capacity of the market to diffuse and minimize discontents constitutes its greatest merit, yet it is apparently the one most completely overlooked by the critics.[5]

· THE INDICTMENT OF CAPITALISM ·

Chapter 6 deals with the many ways in which the state can improve the market's performance. But the political processes are not likely to discover these ways and insist that they be followed if the majority in a democratic society is skeptical of the ethical rightness of capitalism. And this may well be the case.

I propose, therefore, to digress here for a moment to examine three charges presently being leveled against the free enterprise system: a) that it is *immoral* because it depends on competition and self-interest; b) *suicidal* because it is a breeder of wars; and c) *unjust* because of the way in which it distributes its rewards. A fourth charge, that it is inherently *unstable*, unable to provide continuous employment for all willing and able workers, will be considered at a later point.

Is Capitalism Immoral?

The charge that capitalism is immoral should not be taken lightly. If the alternative drives that the critics of capitalism appear to have in mind—altruism and cooperation—are reasonably effective, and are really superior from a moral point of view to competition and self-interest, then capitalism stands condemned. Its admitted productivity will not and should not save it. In the long run a nation's institutions must command respect. But is the charge true?

Admittedly the capitalistic engine requires the fuel of self-interest and the discipline of competition. It will not run on the milk of human kindness. It responds well to the lubricant of persuasion. Altruism and cooperation are poor substitutes. Altruism is an admirable emotion. But it is not enough. Unless it is guided by wisdom and is as concerned for the poorest peasant in India as for the undernourished child next door, it can do immense harm. Unaided, it cannot tell anyone how he can best help his fellows, particularly distant ones of whom he is not even aware. When our sympathy for native migrant workers leads us to close our borders to Mexican peasants we hurt people who are far poorer than those we help.

Cooperation is also an excellent virtue, but it can do harm as well as good. When businessmen cooperate, it is usually to exclude rivals, cut production, and raise prices. When workers cooperate their purpose is to get more for themselves. On page 56 above, competition was defined as "a form of rivalry which makes firms and resource owners offer more for less." A cynic might be tempted to define cooperation as "an effort on the part of firms and resource owners to improve conditions by agreeing to offer less for more."[6]

What is needed in a complex and interdependent world is less "cooperation" and more coordination. Believers in the free enterprise system are convinced that the only way to

coordinate the efforts of people who are scattered over immense areas and unaware of one another's existence is through
the market's signals (prices), which tell people what to do, its
incentive (self-interest), which makes them want to do it, and
its discipline (competition), which penalizes them if they do
not do it.

Viewed in this light competition is an effective and tolerant
disciplinarian. Competition rewards the individual who provides his neighbors *with what they want* yet does not jail
him if he prefers to provide them with *what he thinks they
ought to want*. What it does not do is treat him equally well
regardless of which course he pursues. In societies which accept the way of the market, a man may devote all his time to
composing poetry or painting pictures or preaching to the
souls of men, if he thinks the world will be the better for his
doing so. But he is not entitled to ask the state to force those
to support him who do not like his poetry, who find no beauty
in his paintings, who reject his message of grace. If he really
wants to provide his fellows with what *he* thinks they need,
he must be prepared to pay for his conviction in material
privations. Morality is possible only in societies which permit
people to make decisions of this sort.[7]

Altruism and discipline are admirable virtues. They are
what count when a ship is sinking. They have never been
enough, however, to get people to do day in day out what is
necessary for the good life. The first white settlers in Massa-
chusetts were godly people, bound together by strong religious
ties, isolated in a strange land, surrounded by dangers on
every hand. If any small social group could get along without
the spur of self-interest the Pilgrim Fathers should have been
able to do so. And for a period they tried to. They began by
establishing a common storehouse into which all production
should go and from which all should draw on the basis of
need. The experiment soon had to be abandoned because

it was found to breed much confusion and discontent, and retard much employment that would have been to their benefite and comforte. For the yong-men that were most able and fitte for labour and service did repine that they should spend their time and strength to worke for other mens wives and children, without any recompense. The strong, or man of parts, had no more in divission of victails and cloaths, than he that was weake and not able to doe a quarter the other could; this was thought injustice. . . .

And for men's wives to be commanded to doe service for other men, as dressing their meate, washing their cloaths, etc., they deemed it a kind of slaverie, neither could many husbands brooke it. . . .

After famine and disease had decimated their numbers and "after much debate of things, the Governor (with the advise of the cheefest among them) gave way that they should set corne ever man for his owne particuler, and in that regard trust to them selves. . . ." Every family was assigned "a parcell of land," and when harvest came

instead of famine, now God gave them plentie, and the face of things was changed, to the rejoysing of the harts of many, for which they blessed God. And the effect of their particuler planting was well seene, for all had, one way and other, pretty well to bring the yeare aboute, and some of the abler sorte and more industrious had to spare, and sell to others, so as any generall wante or famine had not been amongest them since to this day.[8]

If we are to have what Adam Smith was later to call "a great society" there is need, as he recognized, for both altruism and self-interest. But if these two powerful forces are to serve society well those who exercise them must be assumed to have knowledge of the consequences of their actions—good intentions are not enough—and must, within reason, be held responsible for the consequences to themselves and to others. In societies based on the way of authority only a few are assumed to be wise enough to be either intelligently altruistic or intelligently selfish. Hence only to them can society safely entrust the enormous powers required to coordinate the activities of the members because only they will be able to resist the temptations of power. Those I have called Liberals, convinced that omniscient saints do not exist, believe that in the long run men will fare better and become morally better in societies in which power is checked through the rule of law, diffused through the institution of private property, informed through prices registered in free markets and exercised by millions of individuals in the daily decisions they have to make as they go about the task of looking out for themselves, their families, and all those falling within the range of their sympathies.

Whether the reader accepts or rejects this idealized picture of the market, he should realize that all its thoughtful supporters defend it, not because of its extraordinary productivity, but because of their conviction that it serves moral ends.

Is Capitalism Suicidal?

The immorality charge still holds if it can be shown that capitalism breeds war. The charge rests on the assumption that the interests of states organized on the basis of private property and private enterprise are inherently and inevitably divergent. But is the assumption true, or is it accepted as true merely because it has been asserted so frequently?

The early advocates of capitalism, writing in the declining days of Mercantilism, were convinced that the intelligent pursuit of self-interest would bring peace, not war. They based their belief on the knowledge that self-interest leads men to specialize and trade with one another, that this trading benefits all those involved, regardless of their places of residence, so long as it is voluntary. Indeed, international trading was regarded as particularly beneficial not only because it widened markets and promoted a more elaborate division of labor, but also because it made available to the specialists in any one country a greater variety of goods than they could possibly secure if all their exchanges were confined within the narrow territorial limits of the nation.

This was a radically new view. From time immemorial men had believed that in any exchange one party gained and another lost. Consequently international trading was peculiarly suspect. The task of government was to see to it that exchanges with foreigners produced a net national advantage.[9] Exports enriched, imports impoverished. The "new economics" of David Hume and Adam Smith in England and of the Physiocrats in France turned this reasoning upside down. Imports enriched. The offset, or cost, was what had to be given up in exchange. So long as the first view prevailed only utopian dreamers talked of perpetual peace. With the spread of the second view more and more people came to believe that free international trading was not only the way to wealth but also to peace. To men like Richard Cobden and John Bright the economic system to which Marx would shortly give the name capitalism seemed not only eminently ethical but the only system which could bring peace to the world. For almost the first time in human history men in high position dared express the hope that their children, or at least their grandchildren, would live in a world in which the clash of arms would be heard no more.

To these early nineteenth-century Liberals, nationalism did not appear to be a threat to peace. It was a unifying force needed to make acceptable the restraints that would assure domestic order with a minimum use of force and would make self-interest serve the general interest, They saw no reason why sovereign nations could not be persuaded to refrain from exercising one element of their sovereignties: the right to exclude from their territories products of foreign origin. Freedom of trade, they were convinced, would create a society of nations so interdependent as to make war unthinkable.

What these optimists overlooked was the close relationship between the nationalism they approved of (patriotism) and the nationalism they deplored (chauvinism). Patriotism is a generous nationalism. Without it a country dies. Chauvinism is bigoted nationalism. It is nourished less by love of country and of one's fellows and more by envy and fear of other countries and other peoples. It is a virus disease which can attach itself to any conceivable sociopolitical system. Capitalism, obviously, has not yet developed immunity to this disease.

But is there any reason to believe that socialism will develop any greater immunity? General reasoning suggests that it will develop even less.

Socialism involves detailed planning and the concentration of power in the hands of a central authority. The United States can opt for socialism, New York State cannot. For the foreseeable future socialism must be national socialism and must be divisive. It is inconceivable that a group of socialist states would voluntarily work out an elaborate territorial division of labor in which each state would specialize on the basis of its comparative advantages. The price signals available to states using the ways of the market are simply not available. In principle, all exchanges with other countries must be planned. International trading becomes again, as in the heyday of Mercantilism, political, divisive, and a source of friction.

Socialist planning tends toward autarchy, and today, after a century of increasing economic interdependence, peoples must continue to trade with one another across national frontiers or millions will starve. Socialists invariably discover, once they start putting their policies into effect, that they have aroused impossible expectations. They are forced to appeal to noneconomic motives, to the patriotism of the people, to the spirit of sacrifice. Now patriotism is a powerful and necessary national cement, but it can be a corrosive solvent of international sentiment. It can only be kept at "sacrifice" temperature by directing it against neighboring nations or subversive elements within the country. The more thoroughly a country's economy is planned the more likely it is that the patriotism needed to "lubricate" the plan will turn into chauvinism.

Imperceptibly socialist planning becomes planning for war, or at least planning in contemplation of war. The national economy has to be militarily strong. The growing autarchy, however, threatens to weaken the military potential, for no nation possesses within its borders all the materials essential for modern warfare. Strategic raw materials and foods must be imported. But this involves a dangerous dependence on one's neighbors. The national plan must be expanded to include control of the areas from which these supplies are normally drawn, or where the normal sources of supply lie within the control of major powers, alternative sources of supply must be developed. Here we see at work the same imperialistic pressures that operated in the age of Mercantilism when the French, the English, the Spaniards, and the Portuguese warred with one another for colonies which were to be the hewers of wood and drawers of water.

So it would be today in a world of socialist states. Only a few would be able to develop autonomous plans. The others would have to reconcile themselves to having their economies planned for them. Hitler tried to subordinate the economies of continental Europe to the requirements of the Third Reich. For a time Russia was able to assign roles to her satellites in accordance with her master plan, but she is now experiencing difficulties as the spirit of nationalism reasserts itself in Poland, Czechoslovakia, Romania, Hungary, and Bulgaria. China is even now trying to force the economies of the smaller countries of the Far East into the framework of her ambitions.

The apparent imminence of war simplifies the planning problem for a socialist government. The production of guns is seen to be more important than the production of butter. It is no longer either necessary or desirable to provide the comforts and conveniences which the people had been promised. And it is precisely when a planned economy attempts to cater to the whims of its citizen-customers that its efficacy is tested. Planning for war avoids this test. It is hardly an exaggeration to say that a government which undertakes to replace the persuasions of the market for the commands of authority requires external enemies.

I am not arguing that socialists are more bellicose than capitalists. Men everywhere long for peace. I am simply arguing that socialism lacks defenses against the virus of chauvinism that are built into societies based on private property and free enterprise. Dissenters in such societies can hire halls, print books and pamphlets—and frequently make money doing so—and demonstrate against the wickedness of a government that makes the toiling masses give their lives to save the foreign investments of a wealthy and greedy minority. Language and acts must be very extreme before the voices of dissent are stilled. Even if a socialist government permitted open protests and made available the gathering places and the necessary paper, print, and presses, dissenters would still lack the persuasive arguments available to their pacifist counterparts in capitalist societies. They cannot argue that the wars they are trying to prevent would benefit a privileged few. The government has a relatively easy time explaining how the territories won by a successful war will make available precious additional resources, permit a more effective division of labor, raise the living standards of all, and bring the blessings of its particular brand of socialism to the misguided brethren who had refused voluntarily to enter into the kingdom. This last argument, in reverse, has, of course, regularly been used by chauvinists in capitalist countries, but it is harder to make it stick.

In *A Study of War*,[10] Professor Quincey Wright, drawing upon ten years of foundation-supported research by faculty members and graduate students at the University of Chicago, flatly asserted that noncapitalistic societies had throughout all recorded history shown themselves to be more prone to war than capitalistic societies. Professor Sorokin's Index of War Intensity,[11] which Wright cites, confirms his conclusion. According to Sorokin, the intensity of war by centuries varied as follows:

Century	12th	13th	14th	15th	16th
Index	18	24	60	100	180

Century	17th	18th	19th	1900–1925
Index	500	370	120	3,080

Had Sorokin calculated an index for the period 1815 to 1914, from Waterloo to Sarajevo, and another for the period from Sarajevo to date, the first would have registered an intensity well below 120 while the second would have registered one vastly greater than the 3,080 shown above. The first period was one in which the role of government was steadily declining while the second witnessed a dramatic and world-wide revival of state interventionism. The margin of error in the Sorokin index is undoubtedly large, yet his findings cannot be brushed aside as meaningless. They confirm what general reasoning would lead one to expect.

Furthermore, most of the conflicts of the nineteenth century were provoked by governments ideologically hostile to capitalism.[12] The spearhead of nineteenth-century German militarism was the Prussian Junker, not the Rhineland industrialist. Japanese militarism found its roots in the countryside, among the peasants and in the army, not in the urban milieu of bankers, merchants, and businessmen. In the United States the War of 1812 and the Civil War were more popular in the agrarian West and the South than in the commercial East and North. British imperialism was supported by the conservative landed aristocracy rather than by the merchants and industrialists. Predominantly agrarian countries like Russia and the Balkan states were more ready to spring to arms than were the more industrialized countries. World War II was begun by the German National Socialists, not by the bourgeois nation of tradesmen across the channel. The counsels of moderation generally came from the business community.

This is not surprising. The ways of the market develop in men of property the habit of reckoning gains against losses. Double-entry bookkeeping, so essential to the capitalist performance, had long since made it clear to the despised bourgeoisie that the surest road to wealth was through expanding their enterprises, not through the expensive and forceable seizure of territories. If capitalism has proved more pacific than other forms of sociopolitical organization, it is in considerable part because capitalists have discovered that war does not pay.[13]

Is Capitalism Unjust?

The third charge remains to be considered: that capitalism is unjust because of the unequal way in which it distributes rewards. This charge too is misdirected. Real incomes in the U.S.S.R. are not only much lower than in the United States but are distributed more unevenly; and inequalities in power are even greater. The really poor countries of the world have never learned to use the ways of the market. They have known from time immemorial both abject poverty and extreme inequality. The gap between the rich and the poor in such countries is far greater than in those which have been willing to use the incentives and accept the disciplines of the free enterprise system. And in absolute terms their poor are much poorer. Capitalism has already abolished the kind of *absolute poverty* that was still taken for granted in the West a hundred years ago and could within the next 50 years in a country like the United States produce enough to provide the very poorest with the comforts and conveniences now enjoyed only by a minority—if the public is prepared to accept the system's disciplines.

Yet capitalism can never abolish poverty *in the relative sense*. Indeed capitalism may have increased this kind of poverty by its capacity to create wants and to make the poor aware as never before of how other people live. This awareness plus the expectations aroused by the market's past performance have made many of today's poor believe that they are entitled now to what the market could easily provide them tomorrow. Hence there is always the possibility that Schumpeter's prediction will prove true, that the majority in a democratic society, concerned with the relative poverty they see in their midst, will support public measures which make capitalism unworkable.[14]

6

Improving
the Market

ADMITTEDLY THE MARKET as described in the preceding chapter was a model, but it was not a caricature. The better its adjustment mechanism is understood, the clearer it becomes that the market cannot operate in a vacuum and that the state can do much to improve its performance by providing the appropriate legal framework.

Liberals of all persuasions agree that the state must maintain order, protect individuals from violence from within and without, and make clear in advance the kind of contracts it will enforce. And most believe it desirable that the state establish a reliable medium of exchange—money—and a system of weights and measures.

· OPTIONAL FUNCTIONS OF THE STATE ·

In this chapter I am concerned with a number of more debatable functions of the state. In trying to decide what attitude I should take toward a public intervention, I find it useful to apply three tests, which can be expressed as questions:

1. Is the intervention consistent with the rule of law?
2. Has it been assigned to the appropriate level of government?
3. Is it consistent with the market's *modus operandi?*

Maintaining Competition

In any society, the first task of government is to maintain order. In a market economy, a task hardly less important is to maintain competition. Government must provide and enforce ground rules. There must be laws to prevent people from getting ahead by fraud. Government must enforce voluntary contracts. The whole complex system of voluntary cooperation depends upon contracts. In general, enforcement is not difficult since voluntary contracts are always advantageous to both sides.

Promoting Knowledge and Mobility

But the state can do much more than maintain order, punish fraud, and enforce competition. It can increase an individual's *knowledge* of alternative opportunities and his *mobility*, or his ability and willingness to act on this knowledge. A reasonable amount of knowledge and mobility on the part of workers, savers, businessmen, and consumers is essential in societies which depend on the voluntary acts of millions of people.

Fortunately the system requires neither complete knowledge nor complete mobility. People spend most of their incomes in much the same way, year after year. This stability in spending habits results in a corresponding stability in the demand for labor and capital. Nor is it necessary for *all* workers and *all* savers to know of *all* alternatives, and to be both able and willing to act on this knowledge. It is enough that some people know and act. Surprisingly small shifts are enough to keep rewards in different fields reasonably equal. This is simply another way of saying that a free enterprise system requires and can have competition, if the majority of the people really want it. It takes a great deal of effort on the part of government to prevent competition from prevailing.

Enforcing Responsibility

The amazing productivity of the free enterprise system is due to the way in which its signals—prices—enable people to coordinate their efforts and reward them for doing so. But this is not enough. People must also believe that its method of coupling rewards to contributions is reasonable in principle and is realized in fact. How closely do rewards measure contributions?

Admittedly the answer is "not very closely." This is due in large part, as will be argued presently, to the fact that governments use their coercive powers to shelter politically powerful occupational groups from the perennial gale of competition that freedom generates. But even if governments did all in their power to encourage competition, there would still be numerous opportunities for people, *as consumers*, to enjoy valuable services without having to pay for them, and, *as producers*, to impose disservices without having to make any compensation. This means that someone is getting something for nothing, a benefit in the case of a consumer, an avoided penalty or cost in the case of a producer. He is not meeting all of his *responsibilities*. Frequently he may not be aware of this, or, aware of it, he may not be able to do anything about it. What is required is a change in the legal framework, a task which only the state can accomplish.[1]

Collective services. Business firms get a return on only such goods and services as can be packaged and sold to those who will pay for them, and withheld from those who can not or will not pay for them. There are other services, equally or more important, that they cannot provide at all, because, once produced they cannot be withheld from those who refuse to pay for them. National defense, the maintenance of order, the enforcement of competition, the prevention of the spread of communicable diseases are services of this sort. They are frequently referred to as *collective services*. Philanthropic groups, relying on voluntary donations, can and do provide some of them, but for the most part they must be provided by the state and paid for by compulsory charges—user charges, taxes, fees, special assessments.

The political processes determine what proportion of society's resources will be devoted to these purposes. About all that can usefully be said here is that the general interest is likely to be best served by arrangements which place the costs of collective services on the people in the areas within which most of the benefits will be realized. The majority in the area will then be able to decide whether they want the services enough to pay for them. Otherwise the political process is almost sure to result in great waste.[2] Mosquitoes are said to grow to the size of horses in parts of New Jersey within easy commuting distance of New York City. It might pay landowners in the affected area to assess themselves a half million dollars annually to keep the mosquito

population down to a tolerable level, but not a million
dollars. They would vote enthusiastically, however, for a
million-dollar mosquito control program if they knew that two
thirds of the costs would come from a state sales tax, and they
would be even more enthusiastically for it if the money came
from Washington.

Diffused services and disservices. More debatable are situations in which private firms, in providing services which are
both packageable and serviceable, provide as inevitable by-
products services and disservices which are so indirect and
diffused that, on the one hand, the firms cannot collect from
the beneficiaries of the useful services, and on the other hand,
the victims of the disservices cannot collect from the firms
responsible for the disservices. If these services and disservices
are substantial, the community would be better served if firms
produced somewhat less of certain goods and services and
somewhat more of others—less of those in which the inevitable by-products are *disservices*, and more of those in
which the by-products are *uncollectable services*. The state
can be helpful in such situations.

A few examples may be helpful here.

Accidents are a cost of production. They can be minimized
but not entirely eliminated. If consumers want coal badly
enough some people are going to be willing to mine coal, and
some of them are going to get hurt. No one can know in
advance who will lose fingers, or eyes, or be killed in under-
ground explosions in any given year. For the entire industry,
however, past records will reveal the probable number and the
probably severity of such accidents. If the firms and the
workers in the industry could agree on the compensation to
be paid for these job-related and unavoidable accidents, the
total annual money costs would be known and each firm could
protect itself by paying an annual premium to a specialized
risk taker, a casualty company. The annual premiums would

be a cost like wages, interest, rent and outlays for machinery, equipment, and supplies, and like them would be paid for by coal users in higher prices. In a society in which the consumer is king he is the one who should pay. The firms cannot pay unless the government shelters them from competition or assumes the costs of compensation. If it shelters them from competition consumers still pay, and pay doubly, in higher prices and in less and inefficiently produced coal. If government assumes the cost, people pay not as consumers but as taxpayers. It is now accepted practice in all modern countries for the state to establish rates of compensation for a wide range of industrial accidents and to require firms, as a condition of doing business, to demonstrate their capacity to pay the stipulated rates of compensation or to take out insurance with a reliable casualty company.

Here then is an intervention that is consistent with the rule of law and with the rationale of the free enterprise system. And it has a further advantage. By putting the costs in the first instance on the firms it makes it worth their while to devise ways and means of reducing the frequency and severity of accidents.

Plant life depends on a thin layer of topsoil, built up over many centuries. Man can destroy it in a matter of years, but he can also rebuild it quickly and at reasonable cost. The rich soils of England and Denmark are almost wholly manmade. No small part of the enormous investment in roads, schools, factories, office buildings, and stores which transformed the United States from a sparsely settled agrarian country into the wealthiest and most powerful industrial nation in the world was made possible by practices which destroyed this fertile topsoil through erosion by wind and water and by leaching. Such practices are now denounced as predatory. Throughout much of our history, however, and subject to the exception noted in the next paragraph, many of them were

economical. At a time when labor and artificial capital were
extremely scarce in comparison with an almost limitless supply of virgin land, the American farmer and lumberman were
converting an abundant asset, land, into another and more
productive asset, capital. These same practices would be
wasteful now when labor and capital have become relatively
more and land relatively less plentiful, and, in fact they are
rapidly being given up.

There is one type of soil destruction which has always been
uneconomical because it imposed uncompensated losses on
innocent third parties. If, for example, a substantial part of
the land in a county is stripmined and no money spent to fill
in the gullies and let nature start her healing processes, the
surrounding farmlands may have to be abandoned. The
county may no longer have a sufficient tax base to support
any local governmental services. Part of the gain of those
fortunate enough to find coal on their holdings was at the
expense of the other landowners in the county. Uncompensated losses also occur when timber is cut from steep slopes.
Rain in time washes away first the topsoil and then the in-
fertile lower strata of earth, destroying in the process both the
uplands and the rich bottom lands.

To some extent, wastes of this sort could be handled by
contract.[3] Where the probability of damages could be determined and the parties causing and the parties suffering the
damages clearly identified, the state could make the continuation of the practices dependent upon evidence that all the
parties involved had reached agreement on the way they
wanted the damages to be handled. In the tree-cutting case,
the owners of the valley lands might agree to pay the upland
owners for the added costs involved in following practices
which stopped erosion; or the upland owners might agree to
compensate the owners of the valley lands for the reduced
productivity of their lands. Such a requirement would employ

the signals which the "idealized" market of the preceding chapter sends forth and, by making costs explicit, would enable the parties concerned to discover a mutually satisfactory solution which in most cases would presumably be consistent with the interests of the whole community.

Many situations of this sort cannot be handled satisfactorily through any conceivable improvement in the laws governing contracts. The damages now going on in some parts of the United States as a result of soil erosion are great and widely dispersed. It is quite impossible to identify all the parties involved and their responsibilities. The state can usefully intervene here and accomplish what competition would force men to do if they were omniscient.

Actually most businesses and most households create some *disservices* of the sort here under consideration. The smoke from factory chimneys, the carbon dioxide from the exhausts of tens of thousands of automobiles have so polluted the air of some of our great cities as to constitute a health menace. The noise of my neighbor's power-driven lawnmower forces me indoors. The fumes from the incinerator in which he burns his trash make me close the windows of my home on a stifling day. His fretful dog wakes me up at night. All these "neighborhood effects" multiply as a society becomes increasingly urbanized. They are among the costs of economic growth.[4] At some point the majority revolts and calls upon the state for relief, and properly so. The Liberal recognizes the need for a public intervention, but he notes that the neighborhood effects vary from community to community and consequently believes that the remedies should be tailored to local needs and handled and financed by local governments.

Up to this point we have been concerned with disservices which households and firms inevitably produce. We now turn to the problem which arises when private businesses produce, as by-products, services which are useful but not saleable. If businesses could collect for such services, it would pay them to expand their operations, and presumably society as a whole would be better off. If these unpaid-for services are substantial, the state, in principle at least, can usefully intervene, to prevent a misallocation of resources—too little in this case, rather than too much.

A well-conceived system of dams generates power, improves navigation, regularizes stream flow, reduces flood damages, and increases land values far distant from the dam sites. A private firm can collect only from those who use power. Government is in a better position. It can tax those who benefit from the other services. A good case can be made for subsidizing multiple-purpose enterprises of this sort, with the state doing the whole job, or subsidizing a private firm to do it. Schools and churches are multiple-purpose enterprises. A road benefits many people besides those who use it.

The market copes imperfectly with situations of this sort. Adam Smith included among "the duties of the sovereign" that of "erecting and maintaining certain public works and certain public institutions, which it can never be for the interest of any individual, or small number of individuals, to erect and maintain, because the profit would never repay the expense to any individual or small number of individuals, though it may do much more than repay it to a great society."[5]

The case for subsidizing multiple-purpose enterprises is clear. But how is the amount of the subsidy to be determined? There is no possible way of putting a dollars-and-cents figure on these unpaid-for benefits. The decision has to be political. It is likely to result in overinvestment unless the people in the area in which most of the benefits will occur know that they will have to pay most of the costs. Otherwise their enthusiasm will be no more significant that that reported in the well-known limerick of

> the old man in a hurse
> Who said, "This isn't so wurse,
> The ride is immense,
> Likewise, the expense,
> But it doesn't come out of my purse."

Welfare services. The term "welfare services" is used here to cover goods and services which private firms can provide but which some people, for one reason or another, cannot buy in "adequate" amounts, i.e., in the amounts public opinion regards as desirable. No matter how affluent a society, there will always be some people in this situation. Unless they are supplied with dollars business firms cannot serve them. To what extent, if any, *should* the state step in and help them? And, if so, *how?* Should families which cannot earn enough to buy "adequate" housing, "adequate" medical care, "adequate" food, clothing, and education for their children, be given the dollars needed to purchase these things, or should these things be provided in kind?

There are sharp divisions of opinion among Liberals as to the correct answer to these questions. One answer starts and ends with a decided "no." The long-run interests of the poor are best served by a state that confines itself to correcting all the market's remedial defects. If it will do these many and difficult tasks well, the economy will grow so steadily and the poor will fare so well that few will need help. The few that do can be sure that the help will be forthcoming from friends, relatives, and the host of voluntary groups that flourish so abundantly in what Richard Cornuelle has called "the third sector."[6] Those who insist that the state take over the task of helping this minority hold their fellows in low esteem. Furthermore, they overlook the fact that the state cannot alter the final distribution of income in the interests of the poor without falsifying the market's signals, dulling its incentives, slowing down its rate of growth, and what is far more serious, without violating the rule of law. Those who advocate the welfare state are in effect advocating the servile state.

Another answer starts out differently but ends the same. The state can alter the final distribution of income in the direction of greater equality without any adverse effects on the market's performance and without doing violence to the rule-of-law presumption against discrimination, but only an all-powerful dictator could accomplish this miracle of moderation. In a democracy the political processes of decision making are bound to carry the redistribution too far.

A third answer comes from those who, wishing to live in a society in which the coercive powers of the state are exercised in accordance with the wishes of the majority, recognize that the majority will probably insist that the very poor be helped by the state. But, unlike their fellow Liberals, they are confident that this help can be given in ways that will actually improve the market's performance without in any way violating the requirements of the rule of law.

Redistribution and the Rule of Law

My understanding of the rule of law is that it frequently requires the grouping of people into classes. Its presumption against differential treatment applies only to those falling within a given class. The rule is not offended by exempting women, children, cripples, and old people from military service. A municipal ordinance requiring young and able-bodied persons to yield their seats to aged and crippled persons in public vehicles is not a violation of justice. The provision of separate restrooms in public buildings for men and women is based on *reasonable* classification. The rule-of-law test of reasonable is simple, though its verification is very difficult: The grouping must be so obviously appropriate to the purpose that, if the matter could be put to a vote, the majority in the groups adversely affected would approve of the differential treatment accorded them.[7]

If this interpretation is correct, a Liberal can logically approve of a grouping of people into classes, based on the size of their incomes, and of a direct and graduated tax avowedly designed to make the final distribution of income more equal. Obviously the graduation would have to be very moderate and the purposes for which the money was spent would have to command the approval of the majority of those liable to the higher rates.

But can the political processes produce such a miracle of moderation? I shall argue later (in Chapter 13) that there is a better chance of achieving this miracle in a country with a federal form of government than in one organized on the unitary principle. Nonetheless, it must be admitted that the historical record gives little ground for optimism. Less than a generation after the passage of the Sixteenth Amendment, and in time of peace, the schedule of rates imposed burdens on a wealthy minority that went far beyond the modest limit set by the rule of law and that they rightly regarded as punitive and confiscatory. Enforcement required the use of what many regarded as tyrannical powers.[8] The belief that the few could be made to pay for almost any services the many wanted encouraged extravagance and that subtle form of political corruption which in the past had been so frequently denounced as "subversive of the federal principle." In brief, the tax, as it has actually developed, appears to be accomplishing all that Marx claimed for it."[9]

Yet the central government in a federation must, if it is to survive in these troubled times, have the power to levy such a tax. If we could start afresh, and with the wisdom of hindsight, it would be relatively easy, I am persuaded, to devise an amendment that would enable the central government to use this potentially destructive instrument of taxation to help the poor, and yet oblige it to do this in a way that would strengthen federalism, improve the market's performance, and make both more secure against demagogic attacks.

But before setting forth this way,[10] something must be said of the complicated ways actually followed in this country for the past third of a century. They are described in the next four chapters. Their shortcomings are now generally recognized. Indeed, they have become so obvious that, at long last, it may be politically possible to try the simpler way hinted at above—what I like to call the Liberal way. It will be described in the last chapter.

7

Protectionism: Old and New

By 1930 THE UNITED STATES ranked first among the nations in industry and agriculture, in its military potential, and far and away first in the level of comfort enjoyed by the broad masses of its people.

· THE ROOTS OF AMERICAN PROSPERITY ·

What is the explanation for this happy situation? It was definitely not due merely to the country's abundant natural wealth and its varied, and on the whole, moderate climates. These resources helped, of course, but there are nations in other parts of the world that are equally favored yet desperately poor. An important part of the explanation, I suspect, is to be found in the impact of frontier living on those who, generation after generation, pushed westward to the fringes of settlement. These men were on their own. They were *free*, free to sink or swim. They were judged by what they could do, not by their family connections. Hard work rated higher than fine manners. The frontier created out of old European stocks a new type of man, a democrat in the social sense, with an enormous faith in his capacity to make his tomorrow better than his today. Progress is not inevitable, but a people who believe in it, who seek guidance in their hopes and in hard work, are more likely to accomplish miracles than a people who believe that their forebears were wiser than they are and that the golden age lies in the past.

Another and equally important part of the explanation is to be found in the nature of the political system worked out at Philadelphia. The Founding Fathers hit on political arrangements which, among other things and perhaps unwittingly, imposed upon the new republic competitive capitalism and assured to businessmen a vast market in which to operate. In 1930 only the United States possessed a domestic market wide enough and deep enough to justify using the many new production techniques which had been made available by recent advances in the pure and applied sciences.

In a free-trade world this vast domestic market would have given us no special advantage. But the war that was to make the world safe for democracy had revived the divisive spirit of nationalism and split the world into petty markets within which, with the single exception of the United States, capitalism could not possibly produce the abundance of which it was capable.

In brief, the exceptional wealth and well-being of the people of the United States appear to have been due to a combination of circumstances: a rugged independence of spirit, a respect for work, a distrust of power, public or private, a belief in progress, an absence of class consciousness, and last but by no means least, a political arrangement under which government could neither erect internal territorial barriers to trade nor appreciably alter the way in which competitive market forces created and distributed wealth and income.

Yet before the economic blizzard that struck the West in the very last days of this third decade had spent itself, it had toppled democratic governments in Eastern and Southern Europe and brought a return of the type of mercantilistic national planning that had made the seventeenth and eighteenth centuries so exceptionally warlike.[1] In the United States it weakened popular faith in federalism and resulted in measures which so fettered capitalism as to lead Schumpeter to predict that it would soon have to give way to what he clearly regarded as an inferior but at any rate workable alternative, socialism.[2]

· THE NEW DEAL ·

The 1932 Democratic party platform[3] gave no hint of the radical changes that lay ahead. It called for:

— "an immediate and drastic reduction of government expenditures by abolishing useless commissions and offices . . . and elimination of extravagance";
— "a cessation of speculation in farm products and attempts to restrict agricultural production to the demands of the domestic market";
— "the maintenance of the national credit by a Federal budget annually balanced on the basis of accurate executive estimates within revenues";
— "a competitive tariff for revenue";
— "a strict and impartial enforcement of the anti-trust laws";
— "unemployment and old-age insurance under state laws."

Franklin D. Roosevelt, the party's standard bearer, as governor of New York, had, it will be recalled, only a few months earlier warned that any attempt by the central government "to make all the laws for the whole nation . . . would inevitably result at some future time in the dissolution of the Union itself." During the campaign he was particularly critical of the deficits incurred by the Hoover administration: "Stop the deficits and let us have the courage to reverse the policies of the Republican leaders and insist on a sound currency." A government which refuses to make sacrifices in its own spending, which "continues to pile up deficits is on the road to bankruptcy."

The platform and the candidate's well-known devotion to federalism led millions of those described in this book as Liberals to vote enthusiastically for the party which had traditionally stood for limited government and had so consistently deplored lavish spending by the central government as a subtle form of political corruption. Yet between Governor Roosevelt's triumphant victory at the polls in November 1932 and his induction into office on March 4, 1933, the public mood had changed, and so too had his views.

In what came to be known as "the Hundred Days," the new President recommended and the Congress rushed through with little or no debate a dozen basic laws which made it clear that the party under its new leadership had cast off its traditional concern for the federal principle. The old name was kept but, in fact, a new party had been born. It was prepared to come to the aid of—and this is merely another way of saying that it was prepared to *protect*—almost any occupational group that found itself in difficulties—and this at the very time it was pledged to a drastic reduction of the high tariffs surroundng the American market.

The greatest contribution to world peace and prosperity that the new administration could have made at that time would have been to adopt a tariff for revenue applicable without discrimination to all countries willing to specialize and trade on the basis of what economists call "the principle of comparative advantage." A step in the right direction was made with the passage of the Reciprocal Trade Agreement Act of 1934. Yet, despite the many negotiated reductions of tariff barriers accomplished under that act, the American market may be as difficult to enter today as at any time in the past. This is due in part to the fact that technological progress has been faster here than abroad, but even more to the fact that the reductions have been highly selective (applying mostly to items not involving any domestic producer interest), granted for only short periods of time, hedged around with escape clauses and preferences to domestic firms bidding on contracts involving public monies (the Buy America Act and the National Defense Act) and so administered as frequently to make the costs of compliance more burdensome than the rates themselves.[4] And the prospects are that we may be even less successful in getting trade barriers down in the days ahead. It is simply not realistic politically to expect a Congress that is willing to protect almost any politically potent occupational group from domestic competition to expose this same group simultaneously to foreign competition.

If the United States is to pursue a genuinely Liberal course internationally, it will have to repeal or modify radically most of the protectionist measures to be discussed in the balance of this book.

· THE UNITED STATES: A NATION OF REGIONS ·

To understand the protectionist effects of these measures a short digression into economic theory will be helpful. From a legal point of view the United States is one vast free trade area within which labor and capital can move at will. From an economic point of view, however, it is more meaningful to regard it as a mosaic of small communities in vigorous competition with one another, and within which people can change jobs without the need for an immediate change of residence. Businesses located in any community produce few of the goods and services consumed locally. Most are brought in from the outside and paid for by what outsiders buy from it. No community can force either capital or labor to remain within its jurisdiction; nor can it force outsiders to buy what its local businesses produce. It can only persuade by lower prices or better services. A community's prosperity depends to a large extent on what may be called its *export* industries.

Intercommunity economic rivalry is so vigorous in the United States that durable monopoly is impossible in the absence of an overt governmental intervention. This is one of the reasons for the two assertions made earlier: a) that the American economy "appears to be sufficiently competitive to justify the Liberal's confidence in it as an allocating and re-warding device" (page 57); and b) that "it takes a great deal of effort on the part of government to prevent competition from prevailing" (page 72).

Intracommunity Wage Differentials

Labor is a community's most important local resource. Local firms bid for workers until all who prefer work to leisure find employment. Firms offer higher wages for skills in short supply and lower wages for skills in plentiful supply. Because of the intensity of competition within and between communities, only firms enjoying some temporary monopoly power can afford to pay more than is required to secure a worker with a given skill. And it is not in the interests of the people in any community that such firms should be required to pay more. If, for a time, there are any profits left over, it is in the interests of consumers everywhere that they should go to those who are in a position to expand production. True, they may not choose to do so. But if they do not, outside capital will in due time come in and the resulting increase in the demand for labor will benefit all workers in the community, not just those attached to the profitable firms. (If this does not happen some form of government-sanctioned or at least tolerated intimidation can safely be assumed).

Losses serve an equally useful purpose. They force the firms involved to improve their methods, shift into other lines of activity, or close down and release resources to firms which can pay the locally prevailing prices for resources. It is not in the long-run interests of a community to protect its unsuccessful firms, or to penalize its successful ones.

Even in the short run it is not in the interests of the poorest paid workers in a community to force firms to pay wages higher than those required by competition. If they do, firms will discharge some workers and they will be precisely those in greatest need of help: the least skilled, the least educated, the old and physically handicapped; and a disproportionate number of these will be members of minority groups. Denying to these people the opportunity to work is not the answer. If most of the people in a community really object to anyone's income falling below some specified minimum, they have an easy remedy at hand. They can tax themselves and supplement the incomes of those not productive enough to earn the minimum. The advisability of doing this is not at issue at this point.

Intercommunity Wage Differentials

Because workers can shift from one job to another and from one employer to another *within a community* without the need for an immediate change of residence, local differences in pay for similar jobs tend to be relatively small. Much larger differentials are needed to induce workers *to move from one community to another*. Capital, so long as it is in liquid form, shows no such local attachment. It will move in response to surprisingly small differentials into any community where law and order prevail and contracts are respected. And when capital moves it reduces the need for workers to move. Some workers, those least attached by ties of sentiment to the places in which they grew up, will move to communities where their skills are better rewarded; some businesses, on the other hand, will seek out communities where the resources they require, including labor, can be had on better terms than in their present locations.

· LABOR MOBILITY VERSUS CAPITAL MOBILITY ·

People are loath to move. Consequently, between communities, differentials in rates of pay for similar work tend to get reduced primarily through capital movements; within communities, primarily through labor movements. Both are needed. In a free society competition encourages both types of movement without requiring either. On balance capital movements would appear to be more humane and hence, public policies, insofar as they are not neutral, should be biased in favor of increasing the mobility of capital and thus reducing the need for people to move.

In his *Inquiry into the Nature of the Good Society* (1937), Walter Lippmann set forth the Liberal position with exceptional clarity:

> On the whole, machines must come to the men, rather than the men to the machines. A civilized life is impossible for nomads who settle nowhere and do not put down deep roots in particular places. For men who have just arrived and will soon depart tend to be crudely acquisitive. They are transients

who have no permanent stake in any community, and there are no ties, other than the cash nexus, between them and their neighbors. They live only in the present, having no ancestral tradition fixed on any place and no care for posterity. The good life finds little encouragement where men do not feel themselves to be links in a chain from the past into the future, where they live from day to day without deep associations and long memories and more than personal hopes. There is no doubt that the industrial revolution decivilized great masses of men when it drew them out of their ancestral homes and gathered them together in great, bleak, anonymous, congested slums.

It follows that if the necessities of a civilized life are to be accommodated with the new economy, the stipulation of the classical economics, that labor and capital must both be perfectly mobile, has to be modified. Capital has to be more mobile than labor, sufficiently more mobile to compensate for the inevitable and desirable human resistance to a migratory existence. This is not to say that all the generations must remain forever rooted in the place where they happen to be. But it does mean that the tides of population must move slowly if old communities are not to be devitalized by emigration and new communities overwhelmed by unassimilable immigration. It should, therefore, be the aim of policy to mitigate this human evil by using social controls to induce inanimate capital, rather than living men, to achieve high mobility. It should be the aim of educational policy to make most men versatile and adaptable in the place where they were born, and of economic policy to make capital mobile.[5]

The New Deal Position

On the eve of the Great Depression, and despite 140 years of complete free trade among the states, community wage differentials within the United States were still very large. Indeed, they were larger than those prevailing in Europe at the time, and they were all expressed in a common denomina-

tor, the dollar, which made them psychologically more apparent than those existing between Manchester, England, and
Naples, Italy. The really low-wage communities were concentrated in the South, the high-wage communities in an area
extending westward from southern New England to the Mississippi, south to its juncture with the Ohio River and then
eastward through southern Illinois, Indiana, and Ohio till it
reached the Atlantic again in Maryland. In 1929 the per
capita nonfarm income in the Northeast was more than five
times the per capita farm income in the Old South—$946
to $183—and almost 80 percent greater than the per capita
nonfarm income in that region.[6]

A proper objective of the New Deal was to bring incomes
in the Old South up closer to the national average. How could
this best be done? By encouraging capital to move into the
Old South? Or by encouraging poverty-stricken whites and
Negroes to move to the great urban centers of the North?

To have deliberately encouraged capital to move into the
agrarian South would have increased the severity of interstate
competition. The political processes inevitably favored the
second solution, and found in Carter Goodrich's *Migration
and Economic Opportunity* a persuasive supporting argument.
The historical record appeared to show that the area described
above—what Goodrich called the Industrial Quadrilateral—
had such a great comparative advantage that "the chances
of future livelihood [there] are in general better than in the
South."[7] The official New Deal planning agency, the National
Resources Planning Board, accepted this thesis.[8] The best
way to relieve the poverty of the rural South was to encourage
migration so that those remaining could have larger farms.
This would permit a shift from corn, cotton, and tobacco to
pasturage and timber raising—from soil-destroying to soil-
building crops. The Board's recommendation was based on
the thesis that the persistence of the industrial pattern demon-

strated that it was an expression of powerful competitive forces and hence natural and destined to continue well into the future. The task of government, therefore, was to help people in the Old South move to jobs in the established industrial areas rather than to promote nonfarm jobs for them in their old homes.

There is, however, a very different conclusion which can be drawn from the same historical record: The high and persistent concentration of industrial jobs in the Quadrilateral was not due to any inherent natural advantage but to artificial obstacles which had weakened the forces of diffusion inherent in the competitive market mechanism.[9] If this conclusion is correct, the Liberal position holds. The new administration in Washington, insofar as it decided to depart from a policy of strict neutrality in its efforts to relieve poverty, should have favored measures which encouraged large movements of capital into the rural South, rather than massive movements of poverty-stricken and poorly educated whites and blacks into the great cities of the North and West.

Spokesmen for business and labor in the Industrial Quadrilateral could not be expected to welcome public interventions which would increase the severity of the competition coming from the South, particularly in view of the new administration's tariff commitment. Though business was out of favor it was able to secure a compromise with which it felt it could live. In return for a pledge to support a lavish farm subsidy program and a law to encourage collective bargaining Congressmen favorable to its interests secured assurances that 1) tariff reductions would be so highly selective as to cause little inconvenience to any important industry, and 2) the new bargaining power accorded unions would be used to bring the wages of firms outside the Industrial Quadrilateral and selling in interstate markets closer to those prevailing within the Quadrilateral.

In brief, the Congress swept into power on the wave of discontent produced by the Great Depression undertook to restore prosperity and to promote the general interest by a system of universal protectionism. The balance of this book is concerned with the consequences of this dramatic shift in policy.

8

Protecting Labor

IN RETROSPECT it is clear that 1932 marks one of the great divides in American history. The election of that year presaged the beginnings of a peaceful revolution which is still in progress. A coalition of special interests—urban workers, farmers, and city bosses—had captured Washington. Spokesmen for organized labor were to play the leading role in this coalition, converting what had hitherto been a predominantly "capitalistic" economy into what Sumner H. Slichter described as a "laboristic" economy.[1]

· IN SEARCH OF A JUST WAGE ·

Actually the power of organized labor had been growing slowly but steadily since Woodrow Wilson had sponsored an amendment to the Sherman Anti-Trust Act designed to ex-

empt workers and their associations from the penalties imposed on other occupational groups whenever their "cooperation" resulted or tended to result in a lessening of competition.
The Supreme Court refused at the time, however, to draw
from the amending declaration, which stated labor was not a
commodity, the hoped-for conclusion that unions should be
given monopoly power. Two measures passed just prior to
the 1932 election proved more successful. The Norris-La-
Guardia Act severely limited the right of management to appeal to the courts for injunctions against anticipated damages
resulting from concerted work stoppages. The Bacon-Davis
Act restricted bidding on public works to firms paying the
wages found to be those prevailing in the communities where
the work was performed.

It is the National Industrial Recovery Act of 1933, however,
that reveals the magnitude of the revolution underway. This
chapter is concerned with this short-lived act and three others
passed shortly after the Supreme Court's 1935 verdict declaring
the act unconstitutional.

The National Industrial Recovery Act[2] required the country's major nonagricultural firms to adopt codes of fair competition. The codes established minimum prices and allocated
output among the members of the "industries" into which tens
of thousands of firms were more or less arbitrarily grouped. In
return for this grant of the power to control entry into their
industries firms had to agree to recognize and bargain col-
lectively with their employees or to accept presidentially
determined maximum hours and minimum wages. No firm
could offer less than its industry minimum. Since most firms
were located in the industrialized parts of the country and
since the codes were drafted by industry representatives, the
wage determinations invariably turned out to be much higher
than firms located in the poorer and more agrarian parts of

the country would otherwise have had to pay. The act admirably protected the territorial status quo. In 1935 it was declared unconstitutional on the ground that it invaded intrastate commerce and delegated excessive powers to the Executive.[3]

To replace it the Congress promptly passed substitute measures designed to get around the Court's objections: the National Labor Relations Act and the Walsh-Healey Act in 1935, and three years later a minimum wage law. Meanwhile the United States Department of Labor gave an interpretation to the "prevailing wage" definition in the Bacon-Davis Act which made it easier to introduce collective bargaining into the building trades.

These four measures supplement one another and must be judged as a whole. After describing each one very briefly, the balance of the chapter will be devoted to an examination of their impact upon the economy as a whole as well as upon their intended beneficiaries.

· THE APPEAL FROM THE MARKET TO THE GOVERNMENT ·

The National Labor Relations Act required *both* employers and workers to deal with one another through unions of the workers' choice, whenever the majority in a plant so desired. Heretofore, with the exception of the brief NIRA era, workers and employers had both been free to decide on their relations with a union.

The Bacon-Davis Act restricted bidding on public works (roads, public buildings) to firms found by the Department of Labor to be paying the wages prevailing in the communities where the work was performed. In similar fashion the Walsh-

Healy Act required the central government to exclude from bidding on public contracts in excess of $10,000 firms found to be paying less than "the prevailing minimum wage for persons employed in similar work or in the particular or similar industries or groups of industries currently operating in the locality in which the material, supplies, articles or equipment are to be manufactured or finished under its contract."

In both of these acts the Congress provided a definition of a "fair wage" similar to that given in the preceding chapter. It was argued there that it was not in the interests of consumers generally or of the workers in a community taken as a whole that firms should be required to pay more than the locally prevailing wage rates since this would silence the profit signal which would in time attract additional capital to a community and thus raise all wages and not just those of a fortunate few.

The minimum wage law, or Fair Labor Standards Act of 1938, prohibits the shipment across state lines of goods and services not specifically exempted, if made by firms employing workers under sixteen years of age, or paying a minimum wage of less than a specified amount per hour for a maximum number of hours per week, with a penalty rate for hours worked beyond the maximum.

To avoid a possible Court veto the act affects only firms engaged in interstate commerce. However, the concept of interstate commerce has been repeatedly and successfully widened until today workers originally regarded as lying outside the reach of the act are covered. The minimum rate has been repeatedly raised.

The Results of the Appeal

What have been the consequences of this appeal from the market to the government? Is the economy as a whole in a healthier state? How have the intended beneficiaries of this legislation—nonfarm workers—fared?

The growth of the American economy over the last 30-odd years has been so substantial that the burden of proof properly rests on anyone who claims that it would have been even greater and the results more satisfactory had these measures not been enacted. Yet this *is* precisely the Liberal claim[4] and since it deals with what might have happened, it depends heavily, though as we shall see, not entirely, on theoretical reasoning. This is inevitable because in the real world so many forces are pulling and hauling at the economy that it is difficult to *prove* anything conclusively by simply appealing to the record.

Let us see, therefore, what consequences theory would lead us to expect from the four measures here under consideration.

The National Labor Relations Act

The assumption behind the National Labor Relations Act was (and is) that employers have more bargaining power than an individual worker because they have more waiting power, that this bargaining power will result in an increase in their profits, not in a reduction of prices to consumers, and that the best way to correct this situation is to require employers to deal with their workers as a group. There is truth but there is also error in this assumption. It denies the effectiveness of competition and it overlooks the fact that the capital, which is supposed to give an employer waiting power, can also be a liability. Most capital is tied up in buildings and in durable and highly expensive equipment. So long as gross earnings cover direct operating expenses and leave something over—something far less than the amount needed to induce the original investment—a firm minimizes its losses by continuing to operate. A legal requirement that it *must* bargain with its employees as a group, that it *may not* go out and look for workers willing to work for what it is willing to pay, can place it in a very weak bargaining position. This is particularly true when business is brisk. In such times it can be forced to accept demands which are quite unreasonable.

An easy way to tell whether a union's demands are reasonable is to note the situation at the gates of a struck plant. If conditions of employment, including wages, are inferior to those generally prevailing *in the locality*, token picketing will suffice. If the conditions are better, more workers will be knocking at the gates for jobs than the firm can afford to hire. Unless government backs the strike, massive picketing with threats of violence will be needed if the workers are to get still better terms. In this case, their demands are unreasonable and should be rejected, even though the firm is making handsome profits. An efficient firm should not be forced to pay more, just as the employees of an inefficient firm should not be forced to accept less. Profits and losses are the market's way of attracting some businesses to a community and expelling others.

A characteristic of American capitalism is the enormous investment in fixed plant. This is what makes the economy so productive, but it also makes it relatively easy for unions to "exploit" business. The Norris-LaGuardia Act (1932), the Wagner Act (1935), certain provisions of the Social Security Act (1935), plus the unwillingness of public officials in some parts of the country to suppress violence on the picket line, have greatly increased this power to "exploit."

Whenever collective bargaining gives workers wages substantially higher than those generally prevailing in the community where they work, "exploitation" may be presumed. All consumers and all workers, except those who do not lose their jobs, get hurt. Consumers are denied the lower prices which competition would eventually give them. Meantime, the increased labor costs lead firms to discharge workers who are not worth the new rates and to substitute machines for men. An artificial increase in wages has the same effect on managerial decisions as a fall in the interest rate. Collective bargaining has speeded up the automation about which union leaders complain.

Unionism is thus responsible for an uncertain amount of unemployment. How much depends at any given time on the capacity of the competitive nonunionized sectors of the economy to absorb those entering the labor market for the first time plus those thrown out of work in the unionized sector; and this capacity in turn depends on how low competition can drive wages in the competitive sectors.

One more point is pertinent to our thesis. If collective bargaining is more widely practiced in one part of a free trade country than in another, and if it results in costs which cannot be offset by improvements in labor relations, investment funds will tend increasingly to seek out nonunion locations. This is what happened following the passage of the National Labor Relations Act. Union strength increased dramatically but unevenly. Southern labor proved difficult to organize.[5] Consequently the flow of investment funds to that region increased. The law thus had the unexpected effect of increasing the severity of the competition to which firms in the Industrial Quadrilateral were exposed and of severely limiting the gains leaders of organized labor had expected. More effective devices were needed to protect labor and capital in the Quadrilateral. The central government's power to spend was now brought into play through the Walsh-Healey Act and a revised interpretation of the "prevailing wage" definition in the Bacon-Davis Act.

The Bacon-Davis Act

As administered, the Bacon-Davis Act requires a bidder on a Bacon-Davis contract to agree to pay at least the local unions' published rates, despite the fact that in many communities these rates are more honored in the breach than in the observance. Furthermore, his chances of getting a contract are small unless he actually employs union labor. As a result, except where Washington provides most of the funds, communities frequently find it cheaper to finance their own public works rather than look to Washington.

Until recently the Department of Labor ignored the fact that the objects of their solicitude, the craft unions, were using their increased bargaining power consciously and successfully in the interests of the dominant white members of their communities. Negroes, Puerto Ricans, and women have been the major victims of these local labor monopolies. In some of the craft unions almost the only way to enter is to be white and to come in through birth or marriage.[6]

The Walsh-Healey Act

This act has had a similarly discriminatory effect.[7] Before an agency of the central government can buy anything in the open market involving more than $10,000, there must be a wage finding. This is a time-consuming and expensive task. Congress has never provided enough to make and keep the findings up to date. Many are made by the interested trade unions and by union personnel.

In general the findings are technically accurate but economically unsound because they follow a fantastic interpretation of the perfectly correct definition given in the act itself. The definition, it will be recalled, ran as follows: "The prevailing minimum wage for persons employed in similar work or in the particular or similar industries or groups of industries currently operating in the locality in which the material, supplies, articles or equipment are to be manufactured or finished under its contract."

The department, however, has successfully ruled that the Congress did not really mean to test the fairness of a bidder's wages against those prevailing in his community. In a masterpiece of obfuscation it held that:

> The prevailing minimum wages for persons employed in similar work is an alternative which stands on its own feet, and even though the term "similar work" is not followed by a comma in the text, the word "or" following the term nevertheless acts as a complete disjunctive; and, because of change in the verbal sequence from a substantive verb ("similar work") to pure substantives ("industries") after the last pure substantive ("groups of industries") cannot strike back to modify "similar work." The present participle ("operating"), on the other hand, readily reaches through "groups of industries" to "similar industries" and to the particular industry because there is no barrier to halt it. Its influence cannot pass beyond this point, however, because the change in the grammatical structure obstructs it.[8]

The prevailing minimum wage is thus held to apply not to a particular firm in a particular community, but to a whole industry, or in a few cases, to all the firms in a large region. Findings are regularly set so high as to exclude from bidding on contracts running into the millions of dollars a host of small firms and many nonunion firms of considerable size located in small communities, despite the fact that they almost invariably pay wages appreciably higher than those generally prevailing in the communities in which they are located.

The act has been made to serve the interests of organized labor and to protect firms located in the larger cities in the industrialized and wealthier parts of the country from the competition coming from the South, as well as from the less urbanized and industrialized parts of the country generally.

The Fair Labor Standards Act

Spending by the central government during the 1930s was too small to offset the adverse effects of the Wagner Act on businesses located in the Industrial Quadrilateral. So, in 1938, the Congress invoked the commerce clause to force firms in the poorer parts of the country, if engaged in interstate trade, to pay wages closer to those union leaders had hoped to impose through collective bargaining.

The Fair Labor Standards Act is popularly referred to as a minimum wage law. Unlike any other minimum wage law in the world, however, it does not reach the really low-paying firms. It applies only to firms involved in interstate commerce —and to them it applies *uniformly*. No account is taken of the size of a firm, of the size of the community in which it is located, of the relationship of its wages to those of other firms in the same locality which are exempted because their products or services do not enter into interstate commerce, or simply for political reasons. For a long time most farm labor was completely outside the reach of the law despite the fact that farm products move in great volume across state lines and farm wages are well below those of the workers covered by the act.

The *uniformity of the rate* is what makes this law so highly protective. If it had established rates that varied by regions, and within regions by size of community, the effects might have been beneficial. In a free society there is need for mobility of both labor and capital. Some workers would have been encouraged to move out of low wage areas but capital would also have been encouraged to move into them. The human costs of adjustment would have been more evenly divided. The decentralizing forces inherent in competitive capitalism would have been somewhat weakened but would have remained powerful. It is worth noting that just such size-of-community differentials were provided for in the employment programs carried on under one of the first of the New Deal alphabetical agencies, the WPA or Works Progress Administration. The country was divided into four regions with five density-of-population classes within each region— twenty in all—and very substantial regional and size-of-community differentials were set.[9]

Had the Fair Labor Standards Act incorporated the same principle, it could conceivably have improved the performance of capitalism by identifying submarginal groups and preparing the way for constructive help. Furthermore, because there is always some waste in any business, a small forced increase in money wages may *shock* a management into doing sooner what competition would eventually force it to do. Fear of loss can sometimes be a greater stimulant to efficiency than hope of profit. A minimum wage geared to local conditions might increase the vigor of intercommunity competition.

But the *interested* supporters of the Fair Labor Standards Act wanted a law that would reduce, not increase, the severity of the competition coming up from the South, as is very apparent from arguments presented in its defense as set forth in the Congressional Record. These supporters knew that a uniform rate would give them the protection they wanted. It was inconceivable that the majority in the Congress—coming as they did from the wealthier, more industrialized, and urbanized parts of the country—would vote for a minimum so low as to have a beneficial *shock* effect on their Southern competitors. The political process thus produced a minimum in the original act (and this was equally true at each revision) well *below* the entrance rates paid by most "covered" firms in the Industrial Quadrilateral, and well *above* those paid by the vast majority[10] of what we referred to earlier as the "export" firms in the poorer and more agrarian parts of the country, i.e., the firms already paying the highest wages in the communities in which they were located and earning the dollars so vital to their welfare.

Each time the minimum is raised these "export" firms must raise all their rates, with at best some slight temporary narrowing of prevailing skill and responsibility differentials. The increase in a firm's total wage bill is always a multiple of the amount required to bring the wages of the few up to the new level. The cost has to come out of the firm's profits. It cannot be shifted because of interstate competition. The market's most important locational signal is made to send forth a false message: the poorer and less industrialized parts of the country are relatively oversupplied with capital; unskilled labor is in relatively scarce supply. The Fair Labor Standards Act thus strengthens the centralizing forces in the market's adjustment mechanism, just as the Wagner Act strengthens the decentralizing forces.

But this is not all. The act has an employment effect as well as a locational effect. Each time the minimum is raised there is some reduction in employment. Invariably those who have the least to offer in the way of skills are the chief sufferers. Since 1939 the minimum has been raised eight times—from 25 cents an hour to $1.60 an hour with temporarily lower minimums in newly covered occupations—and each time unemployment among the most needy and politically helpless increased significantly more than among white male adults, the politically and socially dominant group in this country. The supporting evidence is impressive.[11] In a paper presented in the Fall of 1967 before faculty-student seminars at Fisk University and at the Tennessee Agricultural and Industrial University and at Hampton Institute, Yale Brozen, Professor of Business Economics, University of Chicago, drew particular attention to the impact of minimum wage increases on teen-agers (ages 16 to 19), and particularly on Negro teen-agers. From December 1948 to February 1967 teen-age unemployment had increased in each month following an increase in the minimum wage, while general unemployment sometimes fell and sometimes rose, but always insignificantly. Between the same dates the ratio of teen-age unemployment to general unemployment rose by 50 percent despite the fact that the average level of education of teen-agers had risen considerably over the 18-year period; between 1954 and September 1967, unemployment among nonwhite teen-agers rose far more than among white teen-agers, being 36 percent greater in 1954 and 150 percent greater in 1967. Brozen concluded that the effect of the minimum wage on Negro teen-agers had been particularly "pernicious" because it had denied to so many of them the work experience that would have equipped them to earn more than the minimum in later years.

Since February 1967 the situation has grown worse. In mid-June 1968, unemployment among nonwhite teen-agers stood at 31.1 percent as against 11.5 percent for white teen-agers.

Brozen summarized his findings in the following words: "Minimum wage statutes have benefited a few by slight amounts ranging from the average of five cents an hour increase for a few hundred thousand employees in 1938 and 1950 to 15 cents an hour for two million employees in the most recent legislation. . . . Very slow rates of increase then occur in the years following the jumps. . . . In the interval between the time the minimum is raised and the time productivity catches up with the earlier increase, tens of thousands of people are jobless, thousands of businesses fail which are never revived, people are forced to migrate who would prefer not to, cities find their slums deteriorating and becoming over-populated, teen-agers are barred from obtaining the opportunity to learn skills which would make them more productive, and permanent damage is done to their attitudes and ambitions."

In view of this sorry record, why does the Fair Labor Standards Act continue to command such respect? Why has the Congress shown increasing willingness to raise the rates and extend the coverage? In part, I suspect, it is for the same reason that it has failed to be converted to free trade. Each increase in the minimum wage gives temporary protection to firms located in the wealthier and more urbanized parts of the country. Not surprisingly, businessmen in these areas hail the law as an expression of social justice, even as they denounce as "creeping socialism" other measures that actually improve the market's performance. But what is surprising is the vast amount of disinterested support the law gets. The National Council of Churches in a resolution dated February 1959 tells the faithful that "a minimum wage is a practical and proven means of assuring at least the minimum standard of living necessary for the maintenance of health and decency for family living today." In *The Other America*[12] Michael Harrington endorses the very measures that contribute to the poverty and degradation he describes so eloquently. The National Advisory Commission on Civil Disorders declares that "one way to improve the condition of the unemployed on a national basis would be to increase the federal minimum wage and widen its coverage."[13]

Apparently the adjective "fair" attached to the law induces millions of sincere and generous people to support a measure that is "as anti-Negro in its effects as their intentions are pro-Negro."[14] Regardless of their personal convictions men seeking public office or holding important posts in government know better than to denounce the Fair Labor Standards Act. It was not until after his retirement from the Council of Economic Advisors during the Eisenhower administration that Arthur Burns publicly declared that while the law might do credit to our hearts it "hurts the poor and in general those most in need of our help."[15] And James Tobin of Yale University was no longer a member of the Council (he served in the Kennedy administration) when he pointed out that "people who lack the capacity to earn a decent living . . . will not be helped by minimum wage laws, trade union pressures or other devices which seek to compel employers to pay them more than they are worth."[16]

Most of the billions of dollars spent by the central government over the last generation—other than for its own employees and for what are known as transfer payments (interest on the public debt, social security payments)—must take account of these laws. They reflect the strength of organized labor in the coalition of interests which have controlled the central government since the landslide election of 1932. They have increased the cost of almost every activity involving monies coming from Washington and have reduced employment opportunities for those most in need of help.

In brief the record confirms what theory would lead one to expect. The appeal to the political processes to improve the material lot of wage earners has not accomplished what *disinterested* liberals had hoped for. On the contrary, the most politically and economically helpless groups in American society have been hurt. None of this could have been accomplished without the wholehearted support of the leaders of organized labor, who, despite the lip service most of them pay to the free enterprise system, appear to be genuinely convinced that competition is the enemy of the workingman, that he must be exempted from its discipline on the ground that his labor is not a commodity. Yet clearly the system cannot work under these conditions. Does this mean, as Henry Simons flatly asserted, that there can be no place in a free society for the trade union?[17] We now turn to this question.

9

Protecting Labor (Continued)

THE ANSWER TO THE QUESTION posed at the end of the preceding chapter is clear: the government of a free society can no more deny men the liberty to join unions of their own choice than to join the churches, lodges, and the host of other groups through which they try to accomplish things they could not accomplish singly. The building blocks in a free society are groups, not isolated individuals. A government which banned unions would be a threat to all groups and to the democratic processes which distinguish free from totalitarian societies. Unionism is compatible with capitalism so long as, and only so long as, it does not have the power to shelter workers from the disciplines of competition. Unionism and capitalism are in the same boat. The boat, however, may well founder unless unions can be shorn of the powers which have been so recently granted to them and which they have so flagrantly abused.

· WHAT IS A UNION? ·

A trade union is a multiple-purpose enterprise. It is, among other things, *a business organization*, selling the services of its members on an all-or-nothing basis. Members are committed not to bargain individually. A union can frequently get better terms for its rank and file than they could if they bargained separately. But seldom can it get better terms for all of them. The abler ones could usually do better if they dealt directly with management.

In a very real sense, therefore, a trade union is a *fraternal organization*. Loyalty leads a few, out of concern for older, slower, or less able comrades, to accept less than they could get if they bargained individually. And an employer can afford to offer more than they are worth to some because others are willing to accept less than they are worth.

But a trade union is also an *organization of social protest*. Many great union leaders were convinced that through collective bargaining a better world could be shaped not only for their members but for all people. The belief is genuine and is shared by vast numbers outside the trade union movement. Otherwise unionism could never have attained the formidable power it now enjoys throughout the West.

· UNION POWER ·

Because only about one third of the workers in the United States are organized, the general public underestimates union power. The strikes which annually throw vast numbers out of work and impose losses running into the millions of dollars are evidence of unions' *economic* power.

But the power is also *political*, as the laws described in the preceding pages amply demonstrate. Writing in 1957, Dean Pound of the Harvard Law School declared that American unions had been given legal immunities that permitted them to do with impunity things no one else could do:

> To commit wrongs to persons and property, to interfere with the uses of the highways, to break contracts, to deprive individuals of the means of earning a livelihood, to control the activities of individual workers and their local organizations by national organizations centrally and arbitrarily administered beyond the reach of state laws, and to misuse trust funds.[1]

Amendments to the National Labor Relations Act have reduced some of the abuses described by Pound. Even so, many of our great national unions can and frequently do disrupt the entire economy and cause losses running into the billions of dollars. Admittedly, other occupational groups possess some monopoly power and use it to the full, but the power is never paralyzing. Government has time to find constructive remedies. None of our giant corporations would dare show such contempt for the general public as so many of our unions do repeatedly. Nor would the government dare grant to them the kind of concessions the unions are able to exact as the price for not exercising to the full the powers so unwisely accorded them. Without the aid of competition a democratic society simply can not discipline a large union.[2]

Professor Slichter, whose characterization of the American economy as "laboristic" rather than "capitalistic" was noted earlier,[3] although a consistent defender of trade unionism, expressed misgivings at the way in which "the spectacular gains in productivity . . . made possible by investors, scientists and engineers" were being completely "appropriated by labor which pushes up its wages far faster than the rise in output per manhour."[4] This, he said, was a type of exploitation exactly the opposite to that described by Karl Marx and he asked, "How long will the community tolerate this topsy-turvy system of distribution by which routine workers appropriate the gains made by the risk-takers and the innovators?"[5]

· UNIONS, WAGES, AND COMPETITION ·

In a society as wealthy as ours there is and should be sympathy for the underdog. So long, therefore, as the general public thinks of routine workers as underpaid and exploited and accepts the *union thesis* that they can never get a fair share of the nation's output if they have to compete with one another, just so long may we expect violence in labor disputes and the losses and inconveniences that accompany so many of our major strikes.

Is the union thesis correct? Contrary to popular belief, collective bargaining has probably held real wages down. This is what economic theory would lead one to expect and the historical record confirms it. Over the one-hundred-year period from 1855 to 1955, real wages in the United States advanced faster when union strength was declining than when it was growing.[6] Moreover, the share of the national income going to wage earners has changed very little over the years. One economist has been so impressed by this constancy as to refer to it as "a law of the business universe fully akin to those uniformities in nature with which physical scientists deal."[7] It follows that wage earners have far more to gain materially from the growth of the economy than from collective bargaining.

· UNIONS AND THE RULE OF LAW ·

Until recently one of this country's most cherished goals was "equality before the law." No domestic occupation was to be favored above another. Now, however, members of any overcrowded occupation expect government help. Farmers are paid for not producing. Most professions are allowed to control admission to their "guilds." Unions have been granted powers which no private groups should be allowed to exercise.

The literature abounds with proposals for correcting the present unbalanced situation. For present purposes it is enough to say that the remedy is as simple to state as it will prove difficult to enforce. Unions must again be made subject to the discipline of competition.

· PATENTS AND COPYRIGHTS ·

Wage earners are not the only ones sheltered from competition. Copyrights and patents give writers, artists, and inventors temporary monopolies. Present laws have been on the statute books for a long time. They may need amending. The assumption underlying them is that the temporary monopoly they give encourages creative activity and thus serves the long-run interests of *consumers.* This privilege neither violates the rule of law nor adversely affects the overall performance of the free enterprise system. In fact, it stimulates the rise of real output and fosters variety and diversity.

· OCCUPATIONAL LICENSING[8] ·

More dubious is the shelter licensing gives various occupational groups. The licensing power is exercised primarily by the state governments. Altogether there are today some eighty occupations which, in one state or another, are protected. The occupations range from pharmacists, accountants, doctors, dentists, and psychologists to threshing machine operators, dealers in scrap tobacco, egg graders, guide-dog trainers, pest controllers, yacht salesmen, tree surgeons, well diggers, tile layers, potato growers and hypertricologists (persons who remove excessive and unsightly hair). The mantle of protection is being spread wider and wider.

The ostensible purpose of licensing, of course, is to protect the consumer. Advocates argue—more plausibly in some cases than in others—that a) only those skilled in the licensed arts and crafts know what the standards should be and are alone competent to certify that those seeking entry possess the necessary qualifications; b) those who do the certifying will be as concerned for the customers' purses as for their own; and c) most of their customers are incapable of making intelligent decisions for themselves.

Compulsory licensing has a long history. It was the rule rather than the exception in the Middle Ages. The power of the guilds, in whose interests medieval standards were enforced, had to be broken before the Industrial Revolution could produce the miracles of production which have given to the broad masses in the West comforts kings of an earlier day could not even have imagined. In this area we appear to be reverting not to the age of Mercantilism with its passion for national planning, but to the earlier age of feudalism. And as licensing grows, competition declines, and again it is members of minority groups who are the chief sufferers.

Unless all occupational groups can be kept subject to the discipline of competition, capitalism, the rule of law, and liberty are not likely to survive.

· THE MARKET IS COLOR-BLIND⁹ ·

Unemployment among certain nonwhite groups in the United States is much higher than among whites. Almost to a man members of these groups believe that it is due to the color of their skin. Their bitterness is understandable. What they do not understand is that their difficulty in finding jobs is due less to the admitted disinclination of many whites to work beside persons with dark skins than to the misguided benevolence of the vast majority of the whites. The willingness of this white majority to be taxed to finance foreign aid running into the billions of dollars shows that they are genuinely disturbed by extreme poverty wherever it exists. They want to alleviate it, but because of their distrust of the market, they have put their faith in legislation. Without the approval of this concerned white majority, as well as the approval of the vast majority of nonwhites, the laws that now make it impossible for private business to employ several million people could never have been passed.

For a variety of reasons that have nothing to do with race, the brunt of this unemployment presently falls on those with dark skins.[10] By telling employers that they may not hire workers for less than specified amounts we have created a situation in the private sector in which the number of job seekers exceeds the number of job openings. The businessman can pick and choose and, if he wishes, discriminate against members of minority groups without fear of any financial penalty. He knows that those he refuses to hire cannot offer themselves for less to a rival who does not share his prejudice. Race prejudice has been made relatively costless.

If we had been as concerned for the past third of a century with improving competition as we have been concerned with sheltering occupational groups from its discipline, businessmen could not afford the luxury of refusing to employ workers who would have offered themselves for less. The profit motive is a powerful persuader. It preaches tolerance more eloquently than any churchman, as is evidenced by the speed with which Negroes and men of Spanish extraction have moved into professional baseball and other competitive sports compared with their slow penetration into white-collar occupations that are protected by state licensing laws.

A most ominous feature of the present situation is the public's unawareness of the basic forces at work. Instead of calling on the Congress and the state legislatures to repeal the laws that prevent the hope of profit and the fear of loss from coming to the aid of those most in need of help, the public now calls on these bodies to pass new laws—fair employment practice laws—that establish a presumption of discrimination against any firm that does not employ a "reasonable" number of workers belonging to these nonwhite minorities, even if abiding by these laws requires them to discriminate against more qualified workers belonging to the white majority groups. Having passed one set of laws which made it easy for firms to discriminate against the politically weak, we now pass laws which will force them to discriminate against the politically strong and to lose money in the process.

It is dangerous for a people to try to still a sense of guilt by passing laws they know they will not willingly obey. We tried it with Prohibition with disastrous results. Respect for law suffered a setback from which it has never recovered. We appear to be repeating the same mistake. Government in the days ahead may find it increasingly difficult to perform its first and foremost duty, the maintenance of law and order, without destroying individual liberty.

It is interesting to speculate on what the position of workers belonging to minority groups would be today if the central government from 1933 on, in its efforts to restore employment and reduce inequalities, had pursued policies Liberals have always advocated. Suppose the Congress had insisted that the vast sums it was prepared to vote annually and the still vaster sums householders would spend, should go to firms, foreign or domestic, which offered the best terms regardless of any politically determined test as to the fairness of their wage policies. It seems probable that competition, by this time, would have provided what fair employment laws seek but are not likely to accomplish: jobs for members of minority groups roughly in proportion to their numbers in the communities in which they live and at rates of pay that would in no way be related to race. They would be based solely on the relative abundance or scarcity of the kinds of labor available in these communities.

In brief, we see no reason to modify the conclusions reached at the end of the last chapter. The preference for the political processes of decision making has slowed down the rise of real wages and left labor's share of the national output unchanged; but within the ranks of labor it has reduced the share going to the most needy, and humiliated and dangerously alienated the ethnic minorities who can be most easily identified by the color of their skins.

We turn now to the junior members in the coalition which took over Washington in 1933—the farmers. Their loyalty too had shifted from the market to the polling booth. How did they fare?

10

Parity for Farmers

SOME FARMERS FARED very well as a result of the appeal to the polling booth. But again, as in the case of urban workers, some fared very badly and in general these were the ones in greatest need of help.

The American farm problem is in part a population problem. If, generation after generation, members of an occupational group have exceptionally large families, their incomes will tend to be lower than those in other occupations. On the eve of the Great Depression the net reproduction rate[1] of American farm families was almost 60 percent above the rate needed to maintain the occupation and 80 percent higher than the rate for urban families.[2] The latter were not maintaining themselves.

The biological robustness of the typical farm family was in part responsible for the enormous disparity in per capita incomes at the end of the prosperous 1920s. In 1929 the average annual per capita income for nonfarmers was $908 as against $273 for farmers. The corresponding incomes for the Old South were $535 and $183, for the Far West $953 and $818. The Southeast was *par excellence* the region of concentrated rural poverty. It should be noted in passing, however, that the region's nonfarm per capita income came much closer to the national nonfarm average than did the region's farm average—60 percent as against 20 percent. It was not the region's industries that were responsible for the prevailing poverty. They were paying workers far more than the region's greatest single industry—agriculture. Yet the complaint of business and labor in the wealthier parts of the country was that Southern industry was exploiting Southern labor.

But to return to the farm problem proper, it is clear that the farmers, more than any other occupational group, needed expanded markets for their products, plenty of nonfarm jobs for those least attached to farming as a way of life, and an abundance of land for those wishing to stay in agriculture. And the need was most acute in the Old South.

All three of these needs were reasonably well met down to the end of the nineteenth century. As one of the compromises which held the Union together during its critical early years, the thirteen original states had ceded to the central government their conflicting claims to the vast territories beyond their western limits, with the understanding that new states would be carved out of them as soon as population densities reached a specified level. The country was underpopulated. Every newcomer increased the productivity of those already there by making possible a more elaborate division of labor. Public opinion insisted, therefore, that the public domain be opened up to settlement on easy terms as a means of attracting immigrants. And they came, year after year, by the hundreds of thousands, not merely land-hungry peasants, but also "the tired and huddled masses of Europe's teeming cities." A continent was settled in a century. The 1890 census announced the closing of the frontier. Henceforth, growth of agricultural output would depend on better and more intensive cultivation of existing acreage.

And this is what happened. An era of unprecedented abundance lay ahead. Due to a combination of science and incentives, American farmers were to demonstrate that more and more output could be gotten out of fewer and fewer acres and with a declining amount of labor. The so-called law of diminishing returns, which had given a pessimistic tone to the teachings of the Classical economists, was forced into prolonged retreat. Consequently farmers were going to need as never before the other two outlets: expanding markets at home and abroad for their products and plenty of nonfarm jobs for their children. Yet American farmers, particularly those of the North and West, consistently supported policies which narrowed these outlets.

The high tariffs of the post-Civil War days made farmers pay more for most of the things they bought and get less for most of the things they sold. The Great Depression weaned them from their alliance with the protectionist interests in the business world and induced them to enter into a new alliance—with organized labor—and to support legislation which needlessly worsened the terms on which they exchanged goods and services with other occupational groups within the country.

The gap between farm and nonfarm incomes had widened sharply during the 1920s. It is not surprising, therefore, that the farmer expected the government he had helped elect in 1932 to see to it that he received a "fairer" share of the national income than the market had given him. He overlooked the fact that he had helped manipulate that market against himself. Was he wise now to expect that the political processes which had served him so badly when his voice in Washington had been strong would serve him any better now when his influence there was much weaker than ever before?

The new administration promised in the here and now the income parity that orthodox economic theory claimed competition would *eventually* realize, but only after many adjustments. Income parity is a perfectly defensible goal. Our criticisms of the New Deal farm program will be directed not at the goal but at the means employed. It will be argued that they delayed and frequently thwarted needed adjustments and left us with an agricultural problem that may well be worse than if the central government had done nothing, and almost certainly worse than if it had contented itself with strengthening the competitive forces in the economy in accordance with the pledge in the 1932 platform, and then used its taxing and spending power to help people in need as individuals and not as members of an overcrowded occupation.

· ESTABLISHING PARITY ·

Parity was to be realized by bringing the prices of the farmers' major crops into the same relationship with the things they bought as had prevailed over the five-year period 1909 to 1914. All farmers were to be helped, not just those in need. And once parity was reached it was to be maintained by output restrictions. This was bound to be an expensive and enormously complicated administrative task. For our purposes there is no need to describe in detail the devices invoked: price supports, output restrictions, disposal programs (to the needy at home and abroad), cheap credit, and payments for the adoption of soil-conserving practices.

Farmers, like workers acting through their unions, were expressly exempted from most of the provisions of the Sherman Antitrust Act.

Underlying Assumptions

The success of the program depended on the way in which consumers and farmers would respond to higher prices. Consumers were expected to buy almost as much at higher as at lower prices. In the technical language of economics, the demand for farm products was assumed to be very inelastic. Small reductions in output were to raise prices enough to give farmers more money for producing less goods. This assumption is not true for an industrial product like cotton, except in the very short run, and somewhat less true for food crops in the long run than in the short run. Cotton has to compete with synthetics at home and abroad and with foreign-grown cotton in overseas markets. The parity promised American cotton was bound to result in a substantial expansion of cotton planting in other parts of the world. This part of the farm program went a long way toward pricing American cotton out of its traditional foreign markets. Given time, consumers will adjust their eating habits, shifting from higher to lower-priced foods. Foreign consumers are especially free to shift. They will not buy in a high-priced market at all, if lower prices prevail elsewhere, or at any rate, will buy much less. The availability of alternative sources of supply thus made the foreign demand for America's food crops highly elastic.

So much for the behavior of consumers. What about the behavior of farmers? Here too an underlying assumption proved false. It was thought that prices were so much below costs that moderate increases would not lead to embarrassingly large increases in production. Actually higher prices produced immediate and striking responses which not only increased outputs per acre but speeded up the technological revolution referred to above—a revolution so much more rapid than that prevailing in any other sector of the economy that farmers could earn parity incomes with farm prices much lower than those the government was pledged to bring about. The parity formula thus introduced a highly inflationary element into the economy and required a network of controls and an army of officials to enforce them.

Accomplishments

By the end of 1966 the central government had had a net loss of about $35 billion on these programs. The number of permanent employees in the United States Department of Agriculture has risen from a handful to 115,000. For every 1,000 farmers there are now 33 employees of the central government supervising and regulating them. One quarter of farm incomes now come from governmental largesse. Spending by the Department of Agriculture is running around $6 billion annually.[3] The bulk of the money—some 80 percent —goes directly to a minority, some one million commercial farmers whose incomes in a recent year averaged more than $9,500.[4]

Yet if the subsidy were suddenly cut off this favored minority would suffer severely. Much of the money merely passes through their hands. Earlier owners have reaped most of the benefits in the capital gains realized from the sale of their lands. Since 1935 farmland prices have gone up almost fivefold.[5] While present owners gain little they would lose much if the aids were suddenly cut off. There is no painless way out of the present impasse. Promises have been given, expectations created, and heavy investments made in good faith. The people involved are few in numbers in an absolute sense, but they deserve consideration. But so too do all of those—the vast majority—whose real incomes have been reduced because the nation's resources are not being used as effectively as possible.

Perhaps the chief sufferers of this method of providing parity incomes to farmers are the close to two million subsistence farmers operating dwarf holdings in the nation's poorland areas. The pittances they receive cannot possibly bring their incomes anywhere near the figure declared to be the minimum necessary for health, efficiency, and general well-being. And none have suffered more cruelly than the sharecroppers of the Old South. What these people needed most—poor whites and Negroes alike—they did not get: easier access to nonfarm jobs. What they got were measures that (a) worsened the terms on which they exchanged their small outputs for the products of industry, (b) slowed down the movement of capital into the small towns in their neighborhoods, (c) reduced the number of jobs which businesses in the other sectors of the economy could profitably provide, and (d) concentrated these jobs in places which could be reached only at great monetary and even greater psychic cost. It is much easier for a youngster growing up on a subsistence farm to make up his mind to take a nonfarm job in a familiar and nearby town than it is to look for one in a strange city a thousand miles away.

One further point: our farm program runs directly counter to another national objective, the promotion of world peace and prosperity through the lowering of the high tariff walls which reduce international trade and make it a source of distrust instead of amity. The Reciprocal Trade Agreement Act was designed to give the Executive a powerful bargaining weapon: assured access to the richest market in the world in exchange for equivalent concessions on the part of other countries.

In this bargaining tariff reductions obviously could not be

granted in the case of price-supported crops. And so, in all our negotiations under the Trade Agreement Act, our representatives at the bargaining table have found themselves in a highly embarrassing position. On the one hand, they have to preach the merits of moderate and nondiscriminatory tariffs and the peculiar demerits of quotas and other quantitative restrictions on imports and of export subsidies; on the other hand, they have to explain why the American Government has to maintain duties on its major agricultural crops and sometimes impose quotas in defense of its domestic farm program, and give export subsidies to make sure that it retains its historic share of foreign markets.

This double talk is inevitable. As a major exporter of agricultural products we cannot have, simultaneously, free trade in agricultural products and price supports designed to lift prices within the United States above those prevailing in world markets. Not unnaturally our protestations of devotion to freer trade are taken with something more than a grain of salt. The skepticism is all the more justified because of the many "escape clauses" which had to be inserted into the act to get it through a Congress in which a majority had come to accept the idea that firms in the wealthier parts of the country would be exposed to *unfair* competition if they had to compete with firms in the poorer parts of the country on the basis of wage rates far higher than firms in almost any other part of the world were paying, or likely to pay in the near future.

The reductions in our agricultural exports would have been much greater were it not for the fact that private enterprise was investing heavily abroad and the central government was supplying even more dollars through government-to-government loans and outright gifts. Since 1945 this country has made foreign grants-in-aid well in excess of $100 billion. Never before in history has a great power given so much voluntarily and continued giving so long. It has been politically possible to do this because the vast majority of the American people are disturbed by the abject poverty which prevails in so many parts of the world. But there is, I suspect, another reason—an uneasy awareness that our unwillingness to let the world's poor come to us as in the past, or to allow their businesses to sell to us the products of their low-paid workers may be in part responsible for their plight. And so we give and continue to give. Yet here too, as in our concern for the poverty of the Old South, our policies have not always been helpful.[6]

Our aid to India in money and in food, for example, has made it possible for the Indian Government to build up heavy industries where the rate of return on investment is but a fraction of that prevailing in the light industries providing for the daily needs of consumers, and a still smaller fraction of the return from investment in agriculture. Our food shipments have fed urban workers generally and in particular those engaged in building facilities that will not be fully used for years to come and by then may well be obsolete. For the very reason they helped urban dwellers, they hurt the Indian peasants whose incomes depend on the prices they get for their meager crops. Our food grants may thus have reduced the real incomes of the very poorest among the world's poor. Had our aid from the beginning been directed to improving internal means of transport, to bringing to India the new seeds, fertilizers, and management methods that have revolutionized agriculture in the United States and in the West generally, it is quite possible that the masses would not now be eating less and wearing less than they did twenty years ago.[7]

So here again distrust of the market led to unexpected and undesired results. The political processes, operating at the national level, unchecked by the need to keep the American economy competitive in world markets, more responsive to occupational pressures than to individual needs, produced a silken cobweb of controls which benefited a privileged minority at the expense of the socially and politically most helpless members of the farming community. Several million poorly educated whites and Negroes, tenants, sharecroppers, and owners of dwarf farms received enough to keep them from starving but not enough to *earn* the minimum income a generous public believed they were entitled to.

Agriculture as an occupation and the national economy as a whole would probably be in a healthier state today had the party the farmers helped sweep into power in 1932 been content to carry out the major and entirely orthodox pledges in its platform: "the abolition of useless commissions and offices"; "the cessation of attempts to restrict agricultural production to the needs of the domestic market"; "a competitive tariff for revenue"; and "a strict enforcement of anti-trust laws." A Congress and an administration disposed to work with the market yet keenly aware of the need for immediate and massive relief of individual suffering might then have devised a social security program along the lines suggested by the only unorthodox plank in the Party's platform—"unemployment and old-age insurance under state laws"—that would actually have improved the performance of the free enterprise system and so strengthened the position of the states in the federal union that they could have provided efficiently and economically the many collective services a democratic people may legitimately expect of government.

11

Security
for All

THE SOCIAL SECURITY ACT of 1935 was designed to help individuals because they were in need, and not because they belonged to an occupational group that was in difficulties. And the help was for the most part to be given in money so that the beneficiaries could provide for themselves in the ways that seemed best to them.

The needs covered were those arising from old age, from temporary inability to find suitable work, from permanent physical disabilities, and from being too young to work in cases where parents were unable to meet their children's needs.

130

· OLD-AGE INSURANCE ·

The so-called insurance part of the program for the elderly is administered exclusively by the central government. It provides monthly payments to persons at age 65 who have been taxed long enough in "covered" employment to qualify, on condition that they retire from gainful work, or that their earnings from continued employment do not exceed a specified amount, originally $100 a month, presently $140. The earnings limitation does not apply to persons over 72.

The tax is paid by employers. They may and usually do require their employees to pay half of it. The half paid by employers is presumably shifted as a result of competitive forces and paid by employees in the form of lower wages, or by them as consumers, in the form of higher prices. The self-employed pay the tax directly at an intermediate rate. Earnings above a certain amount—originally $3,000—are not liable to the tax. There is no allowance for debts, for the number of an employee's dependents, and no minimum exemptions. It is a highly regressive gross income tax, taking much more from small incomes than from large ones. Many blue-collar workers pay as much as top executives with salaries running into six figures. The rate started at 2 percent and was scheduled to rise to a maximum of 3 percent by 1949.

Few of those reaching 65 in 1935 and the years immediately following had paid contributions long enough to establish eligibility and fewer still could afford to retire voluntarily in view of the smallness of the annuities to which they were entitled. This was anticipated and as a consequence the rate schedule was expected to produce surpluses in the early years of the program, building up to a total of $65 billion before disbursements to beneficiaries and the costs of administering the program would exceed annual collections. The surpluses were to be invested in United States bonds. The interest earned on these bonds plus the 3 percent levy on payrolls was expected to make this part of the program self-supporting.

Actually events took quite a different course. The scheduled rate increases were repeatedly postponed while the moneys flowing into the Treasury were used (a) in part to meet ordinary government expenses, (b) in part to increase the monthly payments to those already retired, and (c) in part to increase the number of annuitants by reducing the number of contributions older people had to make to establish eligibility.

These liberalizations of the program soon turned the expected surpluses in the Retirement Fund into deficits. Since 1950 the eligibility requirements have been substantially reduced while the tax rate, the earnings liable to taxation, and the benefits have been frequently increased. In 1965 aid in kind was added in the form of hospital and nursing care and annuitants can recover most of their doctor's bills for a small monthly premium. The tax now (1968) stands at close to 9 percent, or more than four times the original rate, and is scheduled to rise to 11.8 percent by 1987. The tax is applicable to the first $7,800 of the wages and salaries of those in covered employment, and the area of covered employment has been greatly extended. Most workers are now liable. The maximum levy comes close to $350.

Some 24 million old people receive monthly paychecks ranging from $55.00 to $160.50 for retired workers without dependents. Total disbursements are running around $28 billion annually. Instead of the contemplated $65 billion surplus —far more than the national debt on June 30, 1935—the Retirement Fund by the end of 1966 was in the red to at least

$400 billion.[1] A 1967 tax increase will decrease the deficit slightly if benefits are not further increased.

This unrecognized debt is a lien on the present and future income of the American people. On whose shoulders will it rest? Who are the beneficiaries?

The beneficiaries are those now over 65. They receive far more than they could have bought from private insurance companies with the amounts they paid directly and indirectly through the withholding taxes levied on their employers during their relatively brief periods in covered employment. The young are paying heavily for the protection they will receive if they reach age 65. Given the rates and benefits prevailing in 1966, a man of 22 taking his first job in that year and earning not less than $6,600 to retirement at 65, could have bought the same protection from a private insurance company and had $38,000 left over.[2]

If there were no compulsion some young people would not voluntarily provide for their old age, and, as in the past, would be taken care of by their children, their neighbors, or the community. To prevent this from happening we have placed an unnecessarily heavy first lien on their current earnings to provide for an old age which some of them will never reach, and not only on them but on the vast majority who would in any case provide for themselves.

In law as well as in fact, these annuities are gratuities.[3] In its brief before the Supreme Court defending the constitutionality of the Social Security Act the government insisted that the word "insurance" in this title of the act was not to be taken seriously, that the central government was not in the insurance business, and that there was no legal connection between collections and disbursements. The collections were taxes and as such available to cover any authorized expenses, while the disbursements were gratuities and as such tax exempt. The Supreme Court accepted this interpretation and thus got around the constitutional difficulty it had encountered in connection with the NIRA.

· UNEMPLOYMENT COMPENSATION ·

Unemployment compensation is handled jointly by the central government and the states. The central government levies a low flat-rate tax on the payrolls of all firms employing more than a specified number of workers—originally eight. Firms with exceptionally good employment records may be granted lower rates. Employers may not, as in the case of the OASI tax, collect any part of this tax from their employees, but this is really irrelevant. Competition presumably shifts the tax onto their shoulders. Like the OASI tax it is regressive. Ninety percent of the tax is credited to the states and is available for paying unemployment compensation, provided the state laws meet standards set by the central government. The remaining 10 percent is used to cover administrative expenses. No state is required to enter the system, but no state can afford not to enter. If it refused, the proceeds of the tax would go to Washington.

All states require some waiting period to establish eligibility and all relate benefits to past earnings. This requirement introduces pronounced regional differences in levels of compensation. In a recent year the weekly average varied from a low of $22.93 in North Carolina to a high of $43.55 in Wyoming. Some states provide for workers' dependents and allow compensation for unemployment due to off-the-job sickness.

To be eligible a worker has to accept suitable employment. He may not be refused compensation, however, for refusing to take a job vacated because of a strike or because the rate of pay or other conditions of employment are "substandard." The interpretation of the vague concept of substandard tends to be determined by locally prevailing attitudes.

· AID TO THE NEEDY ·

There is no needs test in the two so-called insurance programs. The others are jointly financed, jointly administered, and restricted to persons in demonstrated need and falling into one of four categories: dependent children, disabled persons, the blind, and the aged. The states and their local governments are responsible for all those in need who cannot qualify under one or another of the programs covered by the Social Security Act. The 1965 amendment, which extended hospital and nursing care to persons over 65 who are covered by the OASI phase of the program, also extended medical care on a matching basis to the needy aged and to a new category—"the medically needy." The medically needy are defined as persons who are not eligible for relief under any existing welfare program but who have incomes so low that they would become eligible if they had to pay for medical services. The decision as to inclusion or exclusion from the "medically indigent" category was left to the states.[4]

Over the years, Washington's share of the costs of these jointly financed programs has grown, and the matching formulas have been modified in favor of the low-income states. Originally, for example, the central government matched dollar for dollar a state's aid to its needy aged up to a maximum of $15 per person per month. By 1964, Washington was providing 82 percent of the first $35, and then, depending upon a state's per capita income, from 50 percent to 65 percent of anything more a state might decide upon, up to a maximum of $70. In the case of the "medically needy" the central government's share of the total cost varied from 50 percent in the case of the richer states to 80 percent in the case of the poorer states. This type of matching, with the states free to set standards and the central government obliged to pay most of the costs, has encouraged extravagance and made it impossible for the central government to know in advance what it will have to pay for aiding the poor. It is at the mercy of the states.

A state can, if it wishes, put most of the costs of categorical relief on the central government by putting many on the rolls for very nominal amounts. In general the low-income states have done this. In 1967, aid to dependent children in Mississippi averaged nearly one-sixth as much as it did in New York—$9.35 versus $54.50. The cost of operating aid-to-the-medically-needy for the first full year (1966) was estimated at $238 million. Washington's share of the cost of the program for New York state alone exceeded this figure.[5]

The present method of relieving poverty has had another and perhaps more serious consequence. It has encouraged enormous differentials in relief levels, and these in turn have encouraged massive migrations of peoples from the poorer, more agrarian states to the wealthier, more urbanized and industrial states. It has thus reinforced the effects produced by the Fair Labor Standards Act and the other wage measures described in Chapter 8. It is not surprising, therefore, that this country has witnessed over the last thirty-odd years the greatest mass movement of people in recorded history.

Here we have a further example of the way in which the New Deal quest for social justice has run counter to what was earlier called the Liberal approach to the problem of poverty. New Deal wage laws reduced the capacity of the low-income states to attract risk capital, while its method of financing welfare drew people to the larger cities in the wealthier states faster than private enterprise could provide roofs and jobs.

True, the taxing and spending powers of the central government have been used to transfer funds from people in the wealthier to people in poorer parts of the country, but the funds have served primarily to increase consumption and hence have not exerted the same upward leverage effect on incomes there as would an equal injection of risk capital.

· SOCIAL SECURITY AND FEDERALISM ·

The federal principle presupposes a high degree of tolerance. Majorities in one part of a federation must not impose their wills on majorities in other parts, save with respect to those few issues constitutionally recognized as requiring uniform treatment.

The social security program meets this toleration test very poorly. The taxing and spending powers of the central government have imposed upon the states measures which state majorities, acting singly, would never have adopted. Social and economic conditions in different parts of the country are much too different to make it creditable that majorities in all fifty states would voluntarily have accepted a completely uniform set of priorities. The majority of the people in the low-income agrarian states would presumably rank good roads and education (the people in these states generally devote a larger proportion of their incomes to education than do those in the wealthier parts of the country) well above unemployment compensation, aid to dependent children, and their needy aged. The program is geared to what majorities in the urbanized and industrialized parts of the country want. Their excuse—and there is some truth in it—is that interstate competition prevents state governments, acting individually, from providing the kind and amount of welfare the vast majority of their people want.

But there is more myth than truth in this excuse. The people in a state can have as much welfare as they really want. They can have more publicly supplied services if they are willing to get along with less privately supplied services. What they cannot do is place the burden of supporting these public services on those individuals and those businesses that are able and willing to move. Businesses selling in interstate markets, a state's "export" firms, must be kept competitive. Those who own and those who manage these welcome fine schools, excellent roads, and generous and well-administered welfare services, provided their total costs, including local taxes, leave them in a good competitive position. What majorities in the wealthier and more industrially developed parts of the country want are public services which they could afford if they were willing to see their money wages—far and away the largest element in business costs—fall below those in states in which majorities were content with less in the way of public services. By forcing all the states to adopt the same welfare pattern, they believe that in some way or another the burden can be shifted onto other shoulders. This is an illusion. Wages constitute so large a share of the national income that they must of necessity bear most of the burden. But the illusion is so generally accepted that most people take it for granted that it is not only politically difficult—which is true—but technically impossible—which is not true—for one state in a federal union to adopt generous welfare measures unless all the others do the same thing. And so the central government's powers to tax and powers to spend have been employed to accomplish by indirection tasks which were specifically denied to it by the compact of union. In the process the states have become wards of the central government. Still more serious, in its efforts to preserve some remnants of the federal principle (I am referring here to the open-ended matching grants), the Congress has lost control of its own budget. It cannot know in advance how much money will have to be paid out to support a wide variety of welfare programs. It is at the mercy of the political process of decision making which works at the state and local levels under conditions making it unrealistic to expect moderation.

· SOCIAL SECURITY AND CAPITALISM ·

In one respect the performance of American capitalism is better now than in earlier days. The swings of the business cycle are less violent than formerly, but, as will be argued in the next chapter, this improvement has been at the cost of inflation, and the social security program, superimposed upon the restrictive and protective measures described in earlier chapters, has contributed to this inflation as well as to the relatively slow rate of growth and the relatively high rate of unemployment which have characterized the years since the end of World War II.

The Impact on Collective Bargaining

In 1931 the then Sir William Beveridge, a pioneer advocate of unemployment compensation, and later destined to play an important role in preparing British public opinion for the Labour Party's cradle-to-the-grave welfare program, wrote that the difficulties which had beset his country since the end of World War I were due primarily to the behavior of the great trade unions, and that their behavior, in turn, was abetted by the welfare measures adopted during the 1920s. "It is not altogether fanciful to see in trade unionism and the insurance system of today a restriction scheme in which labour is burned in the fire of unemployment. . . . The cause of Britain's exceptional chronic unemployment from

1922 to 1929 may nearly all be summed up under the general heading of growing rigidities—in a world of increasing changefulness."[6]

Fifteen years later, Sir William (shortly to become Lord Beveridge) argued that the way to get union leaders to use their enormous bargaining power with moderation was to guarantee full employment.[7] This was wishful thinking. The record, both in Britain and the United States, suggests that when there are more jobs looking for men than men looking for jobs (Beveridge's definition), it is more rather than less difficult for union leaders to be moderate. With unemployment compensation, with relief to dependents through welfare payments, and with the seniority clauses to be found in most union contracts,[8] the majority of the members of a union, knowing that their jobs are safe, cannot be expected to feel overly concerned about those with low seniority who will get laid off because of a tough settlement. On the contrary, they are likely to suspect a leader who counsels moderation of having sold out to management. He has to get all that the traffic will bear.

The Impact on Employment

In a 1935 message to Congress President Roosevelt declared that the central government "must" and "would quit this business of relief. . . . Continued reliance on relief," he warned, "induces a spiritual and moral disintegration, fundamentally destructive of the national fiber."[9]

Today, the central government is more deeply involved in the business of relief than ever. The number of ADC recipients in New York City more than doubled between 1957 and 1967. Second- and third-generation families are now on relief. Illegitimacy runs high among relief families. Three out of four children on the aid to dependent children rolls in

1967 were reported to be illegitimate.[10] This is not surprising since aid to dependent children constitutes in effect a very heavy tax on marriage for a person with low earning capacity. If a man living in New York City and earning about $3,000 goes through the form of deserting his wife and two children, the wife is eligible to receive relief, in money and services, worth about $2,500. Assuming that the man's earnings were not affected and that his visits to the home were not detected, the couple's total income would be increased by more than 70 percent.[11] Marriage has become a luxury for the poor.

It is also understandable why welfare recipients are reluctant to take low-paying jobs, the only kind of jobs most of them can qualify for. In 1966 a New York City couple on relief with six children could collect over $5,000 a year in tax-free benefits if they were paying rent in excess of $91.95 a month. In that same year the average wage of a factory worker in that city was $5,301.40 *before taxes* and withholdings for social security.[12] In effect we impose a 100 percent income tax on vast numbers of unskilled workers. The amazing thing is not the number now on relief but the number who insist upon keeping off relief. What we have been doing for almost a third of a century now is, to quote again from President Roosevelt's 1935 message, "to administer a narcotic, a subtle destroyer of the human spirit."

These developments are due in part to the wasteful way in which the attack on poverty has been financed and in part to the unwillingness of the majority of us to let wages be determined in the first instance by competitive market forces. We have preferred to turn problems over to the political processes of decision making, which, in a democracy, reflect the will of the majority. And this majority, generous, sentimental, and easily confused by labels, has quite naturally and unintentionally supported measures that have concentrated unemployment on the most helpless members of the politically weakest ethnic groups in our society. It has preferred to support members of these groups in demoralizing idleness in the mistaken belief that if they were allowed to work for what they were worth, the entire wage structure would collapse. And this has happened in a society in which the puritan ethic still makes idleness something very close to sin.

Meanwhile, more and more of those whose earnings place them well above the poverty line wonder whether their efforts are worthwhile. If a worker with four dependents can get tax-free relief worth $1.50 an hour, a job paying $2.50 an hour will seem to be worth a good deal less than $1.00 an hour after allowance for taxes, pay roll deductions for old age, and union dues. Persons wishing to work after age 65 are even more severely penalized. They have to pay the social security tax on their earnings as well as personal income taxes without any increase in their eventual annuities. It would be in the interests of most of them—for there is no greater killer than boredom—as well as in the interests of society that they should continue to work as long as they are willing to accept what their services are worth to their employers. Instead we virtually force millions into sudden and complete retirement at a time when advances in medical science have extended the useful life of most adults far beyond 65.

And the well paid are also beginning to wonder. In their case it is the sharply progressive rates of the personal income tax which are responsible. Despite many loopholes, the progression until quite recently was such that a skilled factory worker could take home after taxes more from his hourly wage than a top executive whose income from investments made him liable to the top income tax rate on his salary. The quest for security and social justice has reduced the importance of work among both the very rich and the very poor, and has pressured millions into premature and undesired retirement.

The market's adjustment mechanism had been badly tampered with during the prosperous 1920s. By the end of the decade the capitalistic engine was knocking badly. The deflationary forces at work had to be halted. Confidence had to be restored. No political party could have refused to concern itself with the plight of the millions who were unemployed through no fault of their own. The remedy many Liberals recommended was generous spending by the central government *coupled with* measures to encourage competition with special attention to making "capital more mobile and men more versatile." The political processes, however, respond more readily to producer than to consumer interests. Spokesmen for every conceivable occupational interest converged on Washington. The coalition which took over in 1933 undertook to restore the economy to health by combining massive spending with a punitive increase in the tax burden placed on a wealthy minority and a network of controls aimed at securing for occupational groups their customary share of the national output. Instead of carrying out the pledges made in the Democratic platform of 1932, a coalition of special interests took over the name of the Party, universalized protection and made it impossible for the private enterprise system to provide the income and the employment which its past performance had led people to take for granted.

There is a certain poetic justice in the way in which the burdens of this new protectionism have been distributed. Had the people in the Industrial Quadrilateral been willing to accept more competition, domestic as well as foreign, employment and real incomes would probably be higher, the future of federalism brighter, regional and racial tensions less, the rate of growth of the economy greater, and the world might well be more peaceful than it is.

From 1930 until our entry into World War II the American economy operated well below full employment. There followed five years of over-full employment. At war's end public opinion, far from being disillusioned by the results of the protectionist measures of the 1930s, took it for granted that they should be continued, and that the government should take whatever additional measures might be required to keep employment at approximately the wartime level.

12

Employment, Growth, and the New Economics

IN 1945 THE UNITED STATES ratified the Charter of the United Nations, provided the Organization with a home, and became its major financial underwriter. In ratifying the Charter the Congress pledged itself to take such joint and separate action, in cooperation with the Organization (Article 56), as might be needed to promote in all member countries "higher standards of living, full employment and conditions of economic and social progress and development. . . ." (Article 55).

Can a democratic government possessed of only limited powers carry out this commitment? Will the attempt to do so jeopardize personal liberty? Before attempting to answer these questions something needs to be said about a relatively new development in economic theory.

· KEYNES AND THE NEW ECONOMICS ·

In 1936 a book appeared with the awkward title, *The General Theory of Employment, Interest and Money.*[1] There was nothing modest about the title. It was not *A Theory*, it was *The Theory*. Nor was its author noted for his modesty. John Maynard Keynes, right or wrong, always set forth his views with clarity, conviction, and with a minimum of the qualifications with which scholars are wont to hedge their conclusions.

The author's credentials were impressive. In 1920 he had written a brilliant analysis and indictment of the economic consequences to be expected from the punitive peace imposed upon Germany.[2] At the time *The General Theory* appeared Keynes was the editor of the *Economic Journal,* one of the oldest and most distinguished publications in its field. He had made an independent fortune by correctly forecasting the gyrations of the world's produce markets, had married a famous Russian ballerina, and was the possessor of a deft pen and a sublime confidence in the power of ideas to shape events.[3] Keynes planned, and from 1921 to 1936 was the editor of, the world-renowned *Cambridge Economic Handbooks* in which members of what was known as the Cambridge School of Economics undertook to popularize the theories associated with Alfred Marshall and A. C. Pigou. In his foreword to all of the early books in the series beginning with those appearing in 1921, we find the following passage: "The main task of the professional economist now consists, either in obtaining a wide knowledge of relevant facts and exercising skill in the application of economic principles to them, or in explaining the elements of his method in a lucid, accurate and illuminating way, so that through his instruction the number of those who can think for themselves may be increased."[4]

The unemployment which plagued Britain throughout the 1920s had shaken Keynes' faith in the adequacy of the policy recommendations usually derived from the Marshallian theory he had expounded so long and so brilliantly. He became convinced that the capitalistic engine could not restore prosperity without a powerful assist from government—an assist that would not be forthcoming until the grip of the existing economic orthodoxy was broken. A new theory was needed to make intellectually respectable and hence politically acceptable the large role he believed government would have to play if the economy was to perform as in earlier days.

Actually Keynes' explanation for his country's persistent unemployment was not new. The Physiocrat Pierre Samuel Du Pont de Nemours had advanced it almost a century and a half earlier.[5] Jean Baptiste Say's refutation—his famous law of markets—had apparently relegated the explanation, like so many others, to the scrap heap of historical curiosities. Keynes now pulled it forth, dusted it off—there is no reason to believe that he realized how completely Du Pont de Nemours had anticipated him—and showed that it was theoretically possible under certain circumstances for a national economy to operate indefinitely at less than capacity.

Had Keynes given his book a less ambitious title, or if he had simply argued that the policies he was recommending were required under the given circumstances, his analysis would have met with little resistance from economists of orthodox persuasion. In 1935 the Delegation on Economic Depressions, convened by the League of Nations, had recommended the use of government deficits as a way of halting a recession.[6] Hitler, following the recommendations of Dr. Hjalmar Schacht, was energetically employing the techniques Keynes was recommending, though for ends Keynes abhorred.

In view of the complete absence in *The General Theory* of any reference to orthodox price theory, it is worth noting that Keynes recognized its usefulness as a guide to proper resource allocation. "It is impossible to think clearly on the subject without this theory as part of one's apparatus of thought" (p. 340). He took its relevance for granted, but believed, and probably rightly, that its introduction into his analysis would complicate his argument and weaken the political impact of his message. His concern was with the immediate. "In the long run we are all dead" was his answer to the plea of economic orthodoxy for more attention to the help traditional price theory could give to policy makers.

The General Theory had an immediate and enormous success. Its timing was perfect. It told politicians, "intellectuals," and the public generally what they wanted to believe. Much good has come from this successful reintroduction into the body of economic thought of the *vue d'ensemble* Du Pont de Nemours had vaguely glimpsed. Yet Keynes' method had an unfortunate result which he recognized in later years. It quite needlessly produced a breach between *micro* (or the traditional) and *macro* (or the new) economics which made it easy for spokesmen for special interest groups to justify policies which he deplored.

Fortunately the breach is rapidly closing. Increasingly economists invoke both the *micro* and the *macro* theories in their analyses of contemporary problems and in their recommendations. When their recommendations differ, it is usually for one of three reasons: different priorities; different attitudes toward the state, and different assumptions regarding the behavior of savers and wage earners.

Keynesian economists stress unemployment, orthodox economists the efficient use of resources. The latter believe that a government intervention which prevents the efficient use of resources—the use of resources in ways that best satisfy consumer wants—is a sedative, not a remedy. To neglect the allocative aspects of a problem is to invite permanent enlargement of the public sector and hence increased consumer dependence on political processes.

At this point the economist's attitude toward the state is likely to influence his recommendations. If he is a Liberal, as the term is used in this book, he tends to be skeptical of the political processes because of their inability to cater to minority interests. Since everyone is in the minority with respect to most of his daily needs, the Liberal would work through the market, looking to the state to satisfy only those wants which the market cannot satisfy at all, or very poorly, because of the existence of substantial indirect benefits and indirect costs. And insofar as he looks to the state, he looks to the lowest possible political subdivision, on the ground that at this level the power to withdraw and the resulting interarea competion force the majority to heed the legitimate interests of minorities.

The third reason—different assumptions regarding the behavior of savers and wage earners—stems directly from *The General Theory* and cannot be disposed of as briefly as the first two.

The Behavior of Savers

In traditional *micro* theory, interest is the price needed to get people to *save*—i.e., not to consume all they currently produce or all that their current incomes entitle them to consume—and to allocate these savings among borrowers. The borrowers are primarily businessmen. They are able and willing to pay for savings because with them they can buy tools (capital goods) and with these tools reduce their production expenses and increase their profits. They would not have to pay for savings if they could get all they wanted from those who are prepared to save at a zero rate of interest. But they cannot. Hence those who will save for nothing or for very little—and many are willing to do some saving on these terms —get as much as those who are induced to save by the prevailing rate of interest. It is this rate that equalizes savings and borrowings and assigns the savings to those who can presumably make the best use of them. The interest rate thus determines what proportion of the nation's resources shall be used to make the additional tools on which future growth largely depends. The lower the interest rate the more businessmen will find it profitable to borrow and the less householders will be willing to divert from current consumption. Changes in the interest rate affect the purposes for which money claims are spent but not the total amount of spending.

In its original formulation this theory assumed that money was completely neutral. It was merely a medium of exchange. The reality was the bartering of goods against goods. This was the assumption behind Say's claim that supply—what is produced by one set of specialists—is always and necessarily equal to demand—what is produced by another set of specialists. The wheat the farmer brings to the market constitutes his demand for the products of the tailor, the blacksmith, and the cobbler. Demand cannot exceed supply nor supply exceed demand since they are but two sides of the same coin.

Long before Keynes economists had recognized that money is not completely neutral. When the farmer exchanges his wheat for money and then for the products of the tailor, the blacksmith, and the cobbler, there will necessarily be a time lag between the act of selling and the act of buying. During this interval an act of saving occurs. It was realized that changes in this time lag would cause changes in the rate of spending, or in the terminology of othodox economics, in the velocity of circulation of money, and hence in the general level of prices. It was taken for granted, however, that in an orderly world this time lag would be fairly stable. There seemed to be no need to reject Say's conclusion, that supply and demand are but two aspects of the same thing, and that, as a consequence, high and persistent unemployment of any resource was unlikely. If a resource was idle it was because its owner had overpriced it. Its idleness was willed, not involuntary.

Keynes accepted the traditional view that the businessman borrows because it is profitable to do so, and that he tends to borrow up to the point at which the expected gain from the use of the last dollar borrowed—he called this the marginal efficiency of capital—equals the actual cost of borrowing the last dollar. So far there was no break with traditional theory. The break came in his treatment of the act of saving. The amount a person saved depended *exclusively* on the size of his income. The larger an income, the larger the proportion that would be saved. It is this adjective "exclusively" that constitutes the break. The old theory recognized that a good deal of saving was a function of income, but not all of it. A 5 percent interest rate might be needed to call forth the first dollar of savings from a poor man, but it was also needed to call forth the last dollar from a wealthy man. Hence changes in the interest rate did determine what proportion of the nation's income would be consumed and how much would be devoted to capital formation.

Keynes asserted that the interest rate has no effect on the amount an individual saves, merely on the amount he *invests*. He has a *liquidity preference* which sets a minimum rate below which he will not lend his savings to others, or invest them in the expansion of his own business. Below this rate he gets more satisfaction from the possession of a com-

pletely liquid asset yielding no interest—and money is the
only completely liquid asset—than from a less liquid asset
yielding some intermediate rate between zero and his liquidity-
preference rate. This unlent part is said to be *hoarded*, to be
saved but *not invested*. It does not provide the purchasing
power firms had counted upon when they made their earlier
agreements with resource owners: with workers as to their
wages, with landowners as to their rents, and with savers
for the use of their savings. If hoarding takes place on a large
scale many firms will be unable to honor their commitments.
It is not now a matter of some firms making profits and others
suffering losses. Businessmen generally are losing money. Even
a zero rate of interest will not induce them to borrow under
these circumstances. The farther interest rates fall below the
level set by prevailing liquidity preferences, the greater the
hoarding and the greater the contraction. A rise in the interest
rate above the prevailing liquidity-preference level is equally
damaging. It brings forth no additional savings; it merely
increases the income of a class for whom Keynes had little
sympathy—the idle rentiers or coupon clippers who take no
risks but live by exploiting "the scarcity-value of capital"
(p. 376).

The Behavior of Workers

Yet hoarding, as Keynes saw it, was not the root cause of
unemployment. It was, rather, the cause government could
most easily handle. Just how will appear in a moment. The
root cause was the behavior of workers at the onset of a
depression. If they were willing to accept sufficiently drastic
cuts in their money wages the recession would be choked off
before it could do any harm. Such cuts would increase the
marginal efficiency of capital, raise the interest rate up to the
liquidity-preference level, and bring savings back into circula-

tion. "When we enter a period of weakening effective demand, a sudden large reduction of money-wages to a level so low that no one believes in its indefinite continuance would be the event most favorable to the strengthening of effective demand" (p. 265). Anything less than this, however, Keynes argued, would do more harm than good. Small cuts would give rise to the expectation of further cuts and thus lead both businessmen and householders to postpone the purchase of nonessentials which might be had more cheaply tomorrow than today. Better no cuts than small cuts.

Some outside event—a war, a natural catastrophe, or a burst of technological innovations—might create a new situation in which borrowers would be able and willing to pay enough to overcome the liquidity preferences of savers. In that event the economy would return to its full-employment level on its own steam. But when this outside force had spent itself, hoarding would start again. This would cause a new contraction that would continue until the national income had fallen so low that the competition of borrowers would raise the interest rate high enough to prevent any of the greatly reduced savings from going into hoards. At this point the contraction would cease, but the economy would not return automatically to the full-employment level. Under private capitalism there could be massive unemployment and poverty for extended periods of time in the midst of potential plenty.

This pessimistic conclusion followed logically from Keynes unrealistic assumptions, and these assumptions in turn derived from his preoccupation with the here and now, with the short run. If the short run is short enough, then his assumptions, as he set them forth very explicitly midway through *The General Theory,* are correct.

> We take as given the existing skill and quantity of available labour, the existing quality and quantity of available equipment, the existing technique, the degree of competition, the

tastes and habits of the consumer, the disutility of different intensities of labour and of the activities of supervision and organization, as well as the social structure including the forces, other than our variables set forth below, which determine the distribution of the national income (p. 245).

Economists of orthodox persuasion do not object to these assumptions *per se*. They are to be found in many standard textbooks and are legitimate and useful devices for showing the steps by which an economy moves toward a position of long-run equilibrium in which, in the absence of some outside force, no resource owner could improve his position by shifting himself or his property to another use or another place. But can policy recommendations be based upon them? Most human action is based on prediction, guided of course by past experience. Much investment, particularly of an innovating character, is anticipatory. It does not wait upon a prior increase in effective demand. It helps create its own demand. And tastes and habits of consumers are anything but static.

Nonetheless it is upon these unrealistic assumptions that Keynes rested his case.

The Remedy: *Fiscal Policy*

There is no reason, Keynes insisted, why the private enterprise system should not operate continuously at its full-employment level, if the government assumed its proper responsibilities. Thanks to its coercive powers it can maintain employment by preventing a decline in the national income (in monetary terms) whenever people's squirrel-like passion to hoard threatens to bring on a recession.

Borrowing and spending. Government can *offset* private hoarding by borrowing and spending an equivalent amount. This will prevent contraction of the money in the monetary circuit, or, in the terminology of the new economics, in effective demand. The government can and should keep this demand at the level which will make it worthwhile for business to offer satisfactory terms to all resource owners. Preferably the borrowing should be from the commercial banks. They can buy the government's bonds without having to reduce their loans to their regular customers so long as their reserves in legal tender money are sufficient to inspire confidence. In effect, they would be lending their own credit. The added cost would be negligible. Consequently, the government can set the interest rate it pays the banks at whatever level it regards as most conducive to the maintenance of full employment.

Since a low interest rate encourages business borrowing without discouraging private saving, Keynes argued that the rate should be kept very low. True, this would involve the "euthanasia of the rentier, the functionless investor," but his elimination would be gradual and would involve no revolution. As he disappeared the state could take over the saving function and continue it until such time as capital had ceased to be scarce. Meantime, with hoarding impossible, the economy would operate continuously at its full-employment level (p. 376).

Taxing and spending. Deficit spending does not prevent private hoarding, it merely offsets it. Government can *stop* it by the appropriate use of its taxing and spending powers. Through progressive taxation and welfare spending the incomes of those who typically save much can be reduced while the incomes of those who save little can be increased. Since cuts in incomes result in even greater cuts in savings, total savings can be reduced to whatever level is needed to bring private hoarding to a stop. The government itself should not hoard—should not operate with a budgetary surplus—as this would withdraw money from the monetary circuit and cause unemployment; nor should the surplus be applied to debt reduction, as the money would go back primarily to the wealthy and again escape from the circuit because of their tendency to save more than they are willing to lend.

In brief, if the new economics is correct, there is no excuse for the business cycle. Through a proper combination of taxing, spending, and borrowing, or fiscal policy in short, the state can maintain whatever level of effective demand is needed to keep the economy operating at capacity, and can promote or slow down growth by encouraging or discouraging saving and investing.

· THE AMERICAN COMMITMENT ·

Can governments guarantee "higher standards of living, full employment and conditions of economic and social progress and development"—to quote again from Article 55 of the United Nations Charter—without infringing on the liberties of their citizens? Most of the governments of the world have answered this question in the affirmative.

The British answer and its pledge had been given in 1944 in a famous White Paper based on the Keynesian prescription. In 1945 the Congress of the United States received an administration-sponsored bill[7] which, had it been approved as submitted, would have committed the government to assure "to all Americans able to work and seeking work . . . the *right* to useful, *remunerative*, regular and full-time employment" (italics added).

The words "right" and "remunerative" in the above statement are italicized because they involve promises which cannot be kept without jeopardizing freedom.

The right to work is very different from the liberty to work. A right is meaningless unless someone has a commensurate obligation, enforceable in law. Only the state, with its power to coerce, can assume this obligation. A totalitarian government can guarantee the right to work, a government of limited powers cannot.

The word *remunerative* was equally dangerous. It defies precise definition. In affluent societies most people live well above the biological-survival level. Consequently they tend to think that there is some level below which no one should be expected to live. It would indeed be an unattractive society in which the majority did not feel this way. Yet the sentiment can do immense harm because there will always be a sizable number of adults to whom employers, for one reason or another, can not afford to pay this minimum. If the state forbids them to work for themselves or for a private employer for what they are worth to him, then the state is morally committed to provide them with "remunerative" employment. Otherwise the word "right" becomes a mockery. Charity, public or private, may provide them with this minimum, but charity can never be a substitute for work.

To carry out this new mandate the bill directed the President, with the aid of a Council of Economic Advisers appointed by and responsible to him, to submit to the Congress in January of each year estimates covering:

(a) the number of people who would be seeking work during the fiscal year commencing six months later;

(b) the amount of investing and spending, by business, by consumers, and by all levels of government, needed to produce a gross national product (GNP) sufficient to provide remunerative employment opportunities for the estimated labor force; and

(c) how much investing and spending could be expected in the absence of new legislation.

Suitable allowances were to be made for the effects of foreign investments and for imports and exports.

On the basis of these estimates the President was to inform

the Congress that the prospective GNP was sufficient, more than sufficient, or less than sufficient to provide the entire labor force with full-time remunerative employment. If he found it was insufficient he was to recommend such changes in existing laws—state and national—and in fiscal policy as would bring the GNP up to the full-employment level. If the estimates indicated that the GNP would be excessive he was to recommend changes in laws and in fiscal policy that would reduce effective demand.

This was an ambitious set of instructions. Can a government which has seldom forecast accurately its own revenues and expenditures be expected to estimate, with even tolerable accuracy, the spending plans of millions of households, of fifty states, of thousands of cities, towns, counties, and special districts, and of some ten million private firms? Actually the margin of error in the grand total appears to have been at least 10 percent in past years, and may well have been larger.[8] Thus if the President announces a prospective 5 percent deficit in the GNP, it is equally probable that there may be an inflationary 5 percent overage. And even when the overall estimate hits closer to the target, the errors in the subtotals may be disquietingly large. In their January 1967 report the Council of Economic Advisers estimated the "real" gain in consumer purchases over 1966 at $20 billion. The actual gain was $12 billion. Consumers were expected to save 5.2 percent of their aftertax incomes; they saved 7.1 percent. Real output was to rise by about 4 percent; it rose by only 2.5 percent. The price rise was expected to be less than the 2.7 percent registered in 1966; it was closer to 3 percent and was rising at an annual rate of 4 percent in the last quarter. Business spending for fixed plant ran more than 20 percent behind the council's estimate. The largest error came in the estimate of the government's own deficit. It was expected to be in the neighborhood of $5 billion at a seasonally adjusted rate for the first half of the year; it turned out to be over $13 billion.[9]

But how can the President know what GNP will be just enough to provide remunerative employment for all able and willing workers? Some level of wages must be assumed. Since the bill required that the disbursements of the central government comply with "all applicable laws," it would appear that at the very least the prevailing Fair Labor Standards minimum would have to be used as the basis for the estimate. Since this minimum was at the time and has always been higher than the wages paid millions of workers not involved in interstate commerce,[10] the President would have to certify to the existence of a prospective deficiency in effective demand and to recommend corrective legislation and additional spending, even though the economy was operating at substantially full employment.

And if the economy was operating well below capacity, what was to prevent employed workers from absorbing the monetary injection in the form of higher wages? If they were able to prevent a cut in their *money wages* when prices and business profits were falling, workers were being discharged, and *real wages* were rising, would they be unable to secure *money wage* increases when unemployment was falling, prices and profits were rising, and *real wages* were falling? Would they stand idly by until the economy had returned to the full-employment level? Keynes assumed that they would.

Is this a realistic assumption? Can a government which promotes collective bargaining, which exempts unions from the discipline of competition, which prices submarginal workers out of the market through unrealistic wage laws such as the Fair Labor Standards Act, the Walsh-Healey and Bacon-Davis Acts, guarantee both full employment and price stability? Will it not be forced to choose between them? Is inflation the price it will have to pay if it uses the Keynesian prescription to eliminate the business cycle? If it chooses the way of inflation, can the inflation be kept within tolerable limits? These are some of the questions many Congressmen were asking when the administration submitted the bill described in the preceding paragraphs.

During its passage through the Congress the bill underwent important modifications and emerged as the Employment Act of 1946. The term "full employment" was deleted from the title and the right-to-work clause and the adjective "remunerative" were struck from the text. The government's responsibility was reduced to the maintenance of "maximum employment, production and purchasing power" under "free competitive enterprise." Most of the other provisions came through and are now part of the law of the land.

Despite the watering-down of the original bill, the law in its present form gives a pledge which neither political party dares ignore. How successfully has the central government discharged this new responsibility? Has the free enterprise system been improved? Is federalism more or less secure?

· CAPITALISM: FREE OR FETTERED? ·

Capitalism is amazingly productive. It could easily bear more than the welfare burdens presently placed upon it, if it were relieved of all the restrictive measures which now fetter it. If we continue along the present course we run the risk of either runaway inflation or drastic regimentation.

Prices have risen almost without interruption since the end of World War II. Between 1945 and December 1967 the purchasing power of the dollar in retail markets was cut almost in half. Yet unemployment seldom fell below the 5 percent level and the interest rate had risen to the highest level since the Civil War. Foreigners hold dollar claims greatly in excess of the gold at Fort Knox and are beginning to wonder whether we can honor these claims. And since 1955 this country's rate of growth (*ca.* 3.5 percent) has lagged well behind the rates of Canada and West Germany (*ca.* 4.5 percent), France (*ca.* 5 percent), and Japan (*ca.* 10 percent).[11]

The creeping inflation is due to the fact that the central government has increased the money supply through deficit financing faster than the private and the public sectors of the economy have been able to increase the supply of goods and services for which money payments are required.

Faith in deficit financing promises to make inflation a way of life. In justice to Keynes it should be recognized that fiscal policy is a double-edged sword, or better, a rapier. In theory, at least, it can reduce purchasing power as easily as it can increase it. It can convert a deficit into a surplus and sterilize it—i.e., neither spend it nor use it to reduce the public debt. It can produce a balanced budget by measures which alter the pattern of spending and taxing in such fashion as to encourage higher consumption or higher investment, depending on whether growth is to be encouraged or discouraged.

A benevolent dictator, willing to follow the advice of the wisest counselors, could not "fine tune" all business fluctuations out of a dynamic economy. In a government with limited powers the chances of success are still smaller. Actually, fiscal policy has a built-in inflationary bias. Spending is popular, taxing unpopular. It is politically much more dangerous for the elected members of the party in power to vote increased taxes than increased expenditures. The temptation is all the greater if the increased spending comes from the banking system and not from real savings.

The politically easy solution, therefore, whenever the public shows signs of restlessness at a quickening of the rate of inflation, is to make token cuts in programs which have not yet had time to develop the vested interests needed for their defense, to issue wage and price guidelines, and to denounce labor and business when they break them, as they must, so long as the flow of new money into the system exceeds the increase in the volume of goods and services to be exchanged for money. The next step is likely to take the form of selective controls: quantitative restrictions on imports, on foreign travel and foreign investments, and ceiling prices on rents, key industrial products, and key wage bargains. Limits have to be placed on profits. Such measures threaten a free enterprise system more than outright inflation. They falsify its signals, generate conflicts of interest that corrupt public and private life alike, and, by preventing private business from competing with government for resources, make employment and growth depend on the continuous expansion of the public sector.

To date the heavy reliance on fiscal policy has introduced an element of uncertainty which has proved destabilizing. The business cycle has not been abolished though it has changed its shape. It can no longer be depicted as a wavelike curve moving along a horizontal axis. Rather it resembles an ascending stairway with employment, output, prices, and incomes rising jerkily, each step followed by a pause.[12] Unemployment remains relatively low, but the human costs are considerable. Instead of imposing the costs of adjustment to changing conditions on an ever-changing group of people, this new type of business cycle management has concentrated them upon (a) retired persons living on their savings; (b) wage and salary workers whose contracts cannot be changed at frequent intervals; and (c) those with low earning power who have been made dependent on relief by "fair" wage laws, collective bargaining, and other restrictive devices. Inflation slowly cuts into the incomes of these groups and leaves them exposed to a continuing and nagging fear of what lies ahead. No small part of the rise in the real incomes of the beneficiaries of the new economics has been at the expense of these disadvantaged groups.

· FEDERALISM: REVITALIZED OR DEBILITATED? ·

Another victim of the new economics has been the federal principle. Through its enormous spending power the influence of the national government now reaches into every nook and cranny of the country. We are witnessing the triumph of the national will over the will of local majorities, the victory of the democratic over the federal principle. Tolerance for local differences has been seriously weakened. The wishes of local majorities are overridden, sometimes *directly* by orders from the center, sometimes *indirectly* and more subtly by the power of the purse.

In such diverse areas as health, education, housing, voting, and employment, local preferences are disregarded. Old people who would still like to work and the most hapless members of ethnic minority groups are the chief victims of this substitution of the political processes of decision making for those of the market. By weakening the decentralizing forces inherent in competitive capitalism, we have needlessly encouraged these people to move into the "great, bleak and congested slums" against which Lippmann warned in his *Enquiry into the Great Society.*[13]

Keynes Once More

Despite the way in which his doctrines have been abused, Keynes was right in holding that government could stabilize employment at a high level through a wise use of fiscal policy. The weakness of the theory, in its original presentation, derived from the exaggerated importance it attached to the maintenance of purchasing power. If an injection of purchasing power is to maintain employment without inflation, and without a continuous expansion of the public sector at the expense of the private sector, the new purchasing power must penetrate promptly into every sector of the economy. The state cannot stand idly by while occupational groups with monopoly power pump it out. This is what has been happening for the last third of a century. The hoped-for employment effect has been transformed into a price effect—a rise in prices harmful to all consumers and particularly harmful to those the new purchasing power was intended to help.

Keynes made it easy for special interest groups to misrepresent his teachings. He was so eager to win converts that he passed over in silence the many political difficulties that might make it inadvisable for a government to use his prescription. At the very end of his life, he reminded his overenthusiastic disciples that the classical teachings "embodied some permanent truths of great significance, which we are likely to overlook. . . . There are in these matters deep currents at work, or even the invisible hand, which are operating toward equilibrium. If it were not so, we could not have got on so well for many decades past."[14]

Under the magic of Keynes' message, which so admirably fitted the needs of a moment, people are forgetting another permanent truth—that power has to be divided and controlled if freedom is to be secure.

13

Summing Up
and Looking Ahead

· WHERE ARE WE NOW? ·

WE ARE NOW BACK to our point of departure. These are exciting and dangerous times. Never before perhaps in recorded history has it been so important to find ways of releasing the enormously productive potential in the free enterprise system —the only form of organization which to date has demonstrated its capacity to operate under the twofold restraints of the rule of law and federalism. Unfortunately, popular doubts regarding its ethical validity have led us to look to the state not only in areas where the political processes of decision making alone are applicable, but also in areas where the market can operate effectively and protect minority interests in a way in which the democratic state cannot.

In Chapter 1 we made a distinction between two brands of liberals—old-fashioned "Liberals" and a new breed of "liberals." We held that both cherish individual freedom, but that the former place more confidence on competitive market forces to promote the general welfare while the latter put greater reliance on the state.

We have argued in the preceding chapters that the growing preference for the political processes of decision making has produced a new and subtle type of internal protectionism which has created regional and occupational animosities at least as damaging as old-fashioned tariff protectionism. By coming to the aid of every politically potent occupational group (instead of trying to help people as individuals) we have barred any really effective move in the direction of the free international trade which liberals of all persuasions regard as the ideal. A government which intervenes to save the X industry from destruction by a domestic competitor can hardly do less when the competition comes from abroad.

By converting a vague concept of a decent minimum income into a wage rate expressed in dollars and cents per hour we have made it impossible for business to employ large numbers of people, and we have concentrated this unemployment on those in greatest need, those who are not presently able, for one reason or another, to earn the minimum we want everyone to enjoy. The majority of us prefer to support unnecessarily large numbers in complete and humiliating idleness, in part, I suspect, because of the fallacious idea that if we let them work for what they are worth they will pull our own wages down.

In making the dollars and cents minimum uniform throughout the country we have reduced the incentive for capital to move and thus increased the need for people to move. As a consequence the migration of people from rural areas to the great cities has been larger than would otherwise have been the case.

By giving unions and other professional associations undue

control of entry into their "mysteries," and by backing them up with state minimum wage laws, we have denied many of these migrants the opportunity to work. To the extent that there is a popular prejudice against them in the communities in which they settle (and there undoubtedly is), we have made it easy for local employers to respect this prejudice, made it, indeed, costly for him not to do so.

Many of our largest cities, located in the wealthiest parts of the country, claim they are now unable to take care of their needy. So they and their state governments look increasingly to Washington for help and are beginning to ask that the grant-in-aid formulas which presently favor the poorer and less urbanized states be revised in their favor. If this happens the billions they say they must have to make their cities fit to live in will increasingly come from the pockets of the people in the low-income states, and more and more of these people will follow their tax dollars. Until Washington stops strengthening the centripetal forces that draw people to our larger metropolitan centers and their environs, and shares its enormous spending power with the states as a matter of right, the crisis in our cities is likely to get worse rather than better.

The young, and particularly those in the lower income brackets, are taxed so heavily (through payroll deductions) to take care of today's old people that they find it increasingly difficult to provide for their own old age. For most it would be folly to try if prices should rise as much in the next generation as they did in the one just past. Today's old people whose thrift enabled them to provide incomes for their last years have seen these incomes cut down by this same rise in prices. Thus, old and young are becoming increasingly dependent upon the state.

Businesses large and small are also coming to feel that the size of their bank balances at the end of the year depends more on what they can get out of Washington than on their capacity to offer more to their clients, the once-sovereign consumers.

All of this has been enormously costly in dollars and cents. It has required a system of taxation which has reduced the ability and the willingness of the well-to-do to save and take risks, weakened the will to work of large numbers who can never hope to earn much more than the decency minimum we want all to enjoy, and appears to have destroyed even the desire to try to find work among many of those who cannot possibly earn this minimum.

Most of the active support for these measures comes from groups that are not really concerned with helping the poor. Most of the votes, on the other hand, come from people who are genuinely and generously concerned.

The very poor of today, both on and off farms, may well be worse off materially than they would have been if, for the past generation, all of us had placed greater reliance on competitive market forces and less on the dictates of our hearts. Certainly the poor are more bitter and more demoralized.

This unwanted outcome of our benevolence suggests that the really poor, precisely because they constitute a small minority, stand to gain more from the way in which householders cast their dollar ballots in the marketplace than from the way they vote in the privacy of the polling booth.

Large as the dollar costs of this quest for social justice have been, the spiritual costs have been even greater. The rioting and wanton destruction of life and property in cities all over the land make it clear that we may be moving in the direction of "a crisis comparable to and graver than that precipitated by the Civil War—'comparable to,' because, like the Civil War crisis, it will take the form of a breakdown of government by discussion, 'graver than,' the Civil War crisis, because it will pit neighbor against neighbor rather than section against section."[1]

More ominous than the actual violence is the growing evidence that increasing numbers in all ethnic groups in the country are coming to conclusions that are palpably false. The conclusion particularly of the dark-skinned among us is that racial discrimination cannot be eliminated by appeal to the political processes since these mirror the will of the majority and the majority is white, that the redress of their grievances can only be had through appeal to their fears, to "massive disobedience," which is a euphemism for violence. The opposing thesis is that the nonwhites are an inherently inferior breed of men, that they are children and must be treated as children, that to spare the rod is to make them into permanent juvenile delinquents.

If these two views come to be accepted, government-by-discussion becomes impossible. Liberty will seem less important than order, and power will go to men resolute enough to establish it and ruthless enough to maintain it. Given the disparity in numbers, this order will be dictated by the fears, passions, and prejudices of the whites. This would be the end of the American dream.

· WHERE DO WE GO FROM HERE? ·

We have gotten ourselves into the present crisis situation through trial and error. If we get out it will doubtless be in the same way.

If the thesis defended in this book is correct, the errors will be fewer and the trials more successful if they are conducted within the limits set by the requirements of the rule of law and the federal principle, and if they use the market's incentive and directional signals. Yet we must not ask the impossible of any of these institutional arrangements. They are means, not ends.

The market is an excellent device for coordinating and rewarding the efforts of those who bring something useful to it. Those who can bring little or nothing of value to it must be taken care of in other ways if they are to enjoy the minimum of comfort and decency the majority of us want everyone to have. Relatives, friends, neighbors, and private charitable organizations can be counted upon to help, but the state too can play a useful role. It cannot make everyone affluent or happy, but it can see to it that no one's income falls below a modest minimum, and it can open the door of opportunity wider than it is at present.

Our objections to so many of the interventions of the past thirty-odd years were not directed at the ends sought—the creation of a more gracious and more humane society—but at the means employed. We argued that excessive reliance on the political processes of decision making had produced costly, complicated, humiliating and self-defeating ways of alleviating poverty. We further argued that there is a relatively simple and direct way which, had it been followed, would not only have abolished anything we would today call poverty, but would also have restored popular confidence in the institutional framework within which freedom finds its surest refuge. We called it the Liberal way.

· A NEGATIVE INCOME TAX ·

The negative income tax recently proposed by Professor Milton Friedman[2] is an imaginative illustration of this Liberal way. Its purpose is to help individuals as individuals because their incomes fall below the level a majority of us want everyone to enjoy and to do it through a straight money income transfer so that those helped may go to the market for what they want and not have to take what the majority think they ought to want.

Under this proposal all single persons and heads of households would have to declare their incomes. Those with incomes above a specified level would pay positive taxes; those with incomes below this level would pay negative taxes, or, in plain English, would receive subsidies sufficient to bring their incomes up to whatever level the Congress regarded as desirable. Assuming that the liability to pay a positive tax began, as at present, on income in excess of $600 per year (for a single person), and that the guaranteed minimum was set at $300, a single individual with zero income would receive a monthly subsidy of $50. As an income rose, the subsidy would decline until it reached zero at the personal exemption level. Thereafter the tax would become positive and would rise to whatever level the Congress regarded as desirable.

This method of helping the poor, precisely because it would help only the poor, would cost substantially less than what is now being spent for welfare purposes[3] and would have a number of other advantages. Friedman cited the following:

> It [negative income tax] gives help in the form most useful to the individual, namely in cash. It is general. . . . It makes explicit the costs now borne by society. It operates outside the market. Like any other measure to alleviate poverty, it reduces the incentives of those helped to help themselves, but it does not eliminate the incentive entirely, as a system of supplementing incomes up to some fixed minimum would. An extra dollar earned always means more money available for expenditure.
>
> . . . The system would fit directly into our current income tax system and could be administered along with it. The present tax system covers the bulk of income recipients and the necessity of covering all would have the by-product of improving the operation of the present income tax.[4]

Economists have long recognized that a genuinely competitive enterprise system could bear the burden of a governmentally guaranteed minimum income for all. Professor Pigou explored the problem and the pitfalls involved in *The Economics of Welfare.*[5] In *The Road to Serfdom*, written toward the close of the second World War, Professor Hayek noted how easily the British economy could provide a guaranteed income if all of the existing networks of restrictions were swept away. "Let a uniform minimum be secured to everybody by all means, but let us admit at the same time that with the assurance of a basic minimum all claims for a privileged security for particular classes must lapse, that all excuses will disappear for allowing groups to exclude newcomers from sharing their relative prosperity in order to maintain a special standard of their own."[6] Professor Arthur Burns followed up his criticism of the minimum wage noted earlier with the admission of the technical feasibility of a guaranteed minimum income for all.[7]

Since Friedman made his proposal it has won the endorsement of hundreds of academic economists and many prominent business and political leaders. Unless one regards any compulsory transfer of income from one group to another as immoral[8] the weightiest objections are political, not economic. Is it realistic to expect the Congress to treat the tax as a substitute for the existing network of restrictive welfare measures? Would the millions who now benefit, or at least think they benefit, from these measures willingly give them up? Would the hundreds of thousands who administer these programs and sincerely believe in them vote themselves out of their present jobs? The risks are admittedly great. But so are risks of continuing along the present course. And these risks could be substantially reduced if the transfer were made part of a package deal involving the repeal, or at least the substantial modification, of the more fettering and protectionist measures described earlier.

The negative income tax, for example, would in effect replace both unemployment compensation and the subsidies going to most farmers and to most of those on relief. It might well pave the way for a revision of the present contributory annuity program that now burdens so heavily the young and low-paid workers generally. It might also make it easier for the government to move in the direction of freer international trade. Consequently a few safeguards might suffice. But there would have to be some safeguards. Unless the "fair wage" provisions in innumerable statutes were eliminated (or at least interpreted in the manner suggested earlier[9]), we would discover that we had jumped from the frying pan into the fire. We would end up supporting in demoralizing idleness even more people than at present, and most of them would belong to the ethnic groups that now bear the brunt of the majority's misplaced benevolence. (For other safeguards, see Appendix.)

If people were again allowed to offer their services for what they are worth to local employers the market's decentralizing forces would be greatly strengthened. A geographical wage pattern would re-emerge, similar to that recognized in the "prevailing wage" requirement under which the Works Progress Administration operated in the opening months of the New Deal.[10] Small communities would become more attractive for businesses that no longer derived sufficient advantages from their locations in our large and congested metropolitan centers to be able to pay the higher rents and higher local taxes associated with community size, and above all the higher money wages competition would compel them to pay. The lower living costs prevailing in smaller communities would attract retired persons and the few who would prefer living on their meager negative income claims than working for the wages employers could afford to pay them. Intercommunity and interregional competition would curb union power and reduce the vast and socially disturbing population movements of the recent past. There would be no mass flight from the big cities. People are loath to move and the big city has many real advantages. Even businesses that would and should eventually relocate would for some time be bound to their present locations by their heavy investments in land and buildings. The bargaining power of workers would be improved. Businesses in the big cities would have to cultivate the ghettos as assiduously as our great corporations now cultivate the campuses of our colleges and universities.

This country faces formidable challenges. How we handle them is of exceptional importance because of the role our wealth and power force us to play in world affairs. Whatever we do affects our neighbors. They too have problems and they may not be able to solve them if we fail to solve ours. Ours, I am persuaded, are due not so much to our vices, of which we have a fair share, as to our virtues. We are all too prone to support any cause with a "noble" label. We suffer from the tyranny of idealism. We tend to forget that good intentions are not enough, that there are seldom quick and easy solutions for ancient evils. We are impatient with the seemingly slow pace at which the voluntary forces in a free society proceed against these evils. Our very idealism blinds us to the virtues of the market and the shortcomings of the state.

Those I have been calling Liberals in this book are as eager as any modern-day liberal to remedy ancient evils. They may, however, have been too patient, too skeptical of finding quick solutions, too little concerned with the shortrun hardships imposed by the play of market forces, and too distrustful of the state. The developments of the last third of a century may have taught both brands of liberals that the ends they seek—and after all they are very much the same—can only be realized through measures which use the coercive powers of the state *and* the persuasive powers of the market in ways that reinforce and do not, as at present, block and frustrate one another.

A final word. Mankind now possesses sources of power capable not only of providing all men everywhere, and within the foreseeable future, with at least a modest existence, but equally capable of making large parts of this planet uninhabitable. The ultimate decision on the use of these powers rests with governments. It is utopian to expect an international organization based on the league principle to keep the peace. A world government based on the unitary principle and possessed of sufficient power to coerce the great states would quickly become a tyranny. Perhaps the only way out from under the dark cloud of destruction now hanging over all mankind is through the gradual and peaceful coming together, in a larger federal union, of all countries that accept the rule of law and are able and willing to abide by the restraints it places on their sovereignty.

Can we in the United States enter such a union if we do not first show that we are aware of the damage our quest for social justice has done to the federal principle and then demonstrate that we have the initiative, the imagination, and the political courage to do whatever is necessary to make the states again a vital force in the country where the federal principle was first tried and where it operated so long and so successfully?

Federalism and capitalism are means, not ends. Neither is perfect. But in a world where men are neither very wise nor very virtuous, they may well be the only means now available for protecting the liberty and the dignity of the individual and for bringing peace and some modest degree of comfort to a divided and troubled world.

Appendix

Admittedly the underwriting of a universal minimum income is dangerous business. Only the central government can take on such task. What, it may well be asked, is to prevent the political processes operating at the national level from gradually pushing the minimum to a level that destroys incentives and stalls the capitalistic engine? If that happened, a negative income tax, or any other proposal for establishing a floor below which no one's income could fall, would prove to have been a shortsighted device for making poverty more acceptable by making everyone poor.

The package deal suggested in the body of this chapter might not be enough to avert this danger. Fortunately there are several additional safeguards[1] available to a society organized on the federal principle. Three might well suffice. The first would be the requirement of a rigid and specified spread between the lowest and the highest positive rates of the personal income tax. The second would be a requirement that the states be given a share in the proceeds of the tax as a

176

right and without strings attached. The third would restrict the right to vote in national elections to those paying a direct tax to the central government. To be effective these safeguards should be anchored in the Constitution.

The rigid-spread requirement. This requirement would effectively dampen enthusiasm for pushing progression to punitive heights. With a maximum spread of 25 percentage points, for example, a top rate of 91 percent, such as prevailed for many years, would require a beginning rate of 66 percent. The majority could not burden a wealthy minority without burdening themselves; nor unburden themselves without unburdening this same minority. The resulting pressure to keep the beginning rate low would not appreciably reduce the productivity of the tax. The higher rates invite evasion, produce little in the way of revenue, much in the way of resentment, and are only tolerable because of the many loopholes their presence requires. In 1959 a flat 23.5 percent tax would have yielded as much revenue as a graduated tax beginning at 20 percent, reaching 50 percent on the excess of taxable income over $18,000, for a single person, and finally reaching the 91 percent referred to immediately above.

The revenue-sharing requirement. The requirement that a specified fraction of the total revenues of the central government be returned to the states would have a number of advantages, particularly if, as I would hope, the return favored the low-income states. First, it would satisfy the same generous egalitarian strain in American democracy which has made us willing to give aid running into the billions of dollars to the governments of the so-called underdeveloped countries, and with less strings than those attached to the billions given to our own states under the matching grants described earlier. Second, it would make it easier politically for the central government to withdraw from existing domestic welfare programs. Third, it would deprive the states of the excuse they now have for not doing the many things their local majorities may reasonably expect. Fourth, it would increase the likelihood that the income guarantee would be kept low. Voters in the wealthier states would hardly favor a minimum that exempted the majority of the people in the poorer states from liability to pay any direct tax to the central government. On the other hand, the wealthier states could, and doubtless most of them would, supplement the negative income tax from their own revenues. Fifth, it would increase the likelihood that the upper rates of the personal income tax would be kept moderate, except in great emergencies.

Finally a compulsory tax-sharing requirement would create an additional and presumably wholesome conflict of interest between two power centers. Members of the Congress would weigh the advantages of having plenty of money to spend on tasks clearly assigned to the central government against those to be expected from tax reductions. Their interest in providing more money for state and local officials to spend would hardly be more than tepid. Conversely, men elected to state and local offices would want the Congress to tax heavily, spend frugally, and distribute lavishly. Every economy Washington could effect would increase the amount of money they would have to spend in their own states and according to their own priorities. Even if local pressures kept the taxes raised by the central government high and total public spending high, the proportion spent by the states would be greater. Hence the spending would reflect more accurately than at present what local majorities wanted and would presumably be spent with more attention to efficiency because of the necessity for keeping the economies of the states competitive.

The right-to-vote requirement. Limiting the right to vote in national elections to those paying a direct tax to the central government would obviously reduce the risk that income redistribution would be carried to excessive lengths. But would it be undemocratic? Would it violate the rule-of-law presumption that the basic laws of a society should reflect the wisdom and the will of the majority?

Democracy does not require universal suffrage. Switzerland is surely a democratic country, despite the fact that the women cannot vote. In many localities in the United States only property owners are allowed to vote on certain issues. Nor is the rule of law violated by reasonable restrictions on the suffrage. The most ardent advocate of universal suffrage does not insist that babes-in-arms, imbeciles, and inmates of prisons be brought to the polls to vote. All the rule requires is that exclusions be "reasonable" and equitably enforced. There is nothing inequitable in a law that requires those to abstain from voting on a measure that is for their exclusive benefit. It is one thing for the many to tax themselves to help the few; it is quite another thing for them to impose burdens on the few, simply because they have the power. If the majority in this country should desire to attack the problem of poverty through some form of guaranteed minimum income, it would seem both prudent and equitable to limit the right to vote in national elections to those who had paid at least a nominal direct tax to the central government in the preceding year. In any event the vast majority of adults would be eligible to vote in national elections. And the Internal Revenue Service's task would be simplified. Large numbers with incomes just above the personal exemption level would realize that the cost of income evasion was the loss of the right to vote.

If the states could levy steeply graduated taxes on incomes, the case for restricting the suffrage in state elections would be equally valid. But they cannot. The wealthy few are protected by their power to withdraw themselves and their resources from the reach of a state that treats them harshly. All, rich and poor, have to contribute roughly in proportion to their incomes. In state and local elections, therefore, the presumption is in favor of universal suffrage. The Congress and the Supreme Court of the United States can and should intervene if a state denies the right to vote on any such irrelevant ground as race, creed, or color, or inequitably administers an otherwise reasonable requirement.

It would probably be impossible at the present time to amend the American Constitution along lines here suggested. But the time may come when the dangers threatening the nations of the free world may make them want to form a wider federal union. The obstacles would be formidable. The prospects of getting the wealthier states to enter such a union would be greatly increased if it was understood from the beginning that safeguards such as these would be incorporated into the original compact.

Notes

CHAPTER 1

1. Hans Kohn, *Nationalism: Its Meaning and History* (New York: Van Nostrand, 1955).
2. Bronislaw Malinowski, "An Anthropological Analysis of War," *The American Journal of Sociology,* 46 (January 1941), p. 549.
3. *Essays in Freedom and Power* (New York: American Book Co., 1955), p. 335.
4. *The Writings of Abraham Lincoln,* ed. A. B. Lapsley (New York: G. P. Putnam's Sons, 1906), VII, p. 121.
5. In *Two Concepts of Liberty* (Oxford: The Clarendon Press, 1958) Sir Isaiah Berlin brings out this distinction very clearly: "What members of primitive societies want, as often as not, is simple recognition. . . . To be ruled, educated, guided with however light a hand, is regarded as being not fully human, and therefore not quite fully free." This desire is so intense that "it is possible for men, while submitting to the authority of dictators, to claim that this in some sense liberates them" (pp. 40–43).
6. Quoted by Erich Fromm in *Marx's Concept of Man* (New York: Frederick Ungar, 1961), pp. 37–38.
7. *Ibid.,* p. 59.
8. *Ibid.,* p. 42
9. *Ibid.,* p. 39
10. *The Democratic Way of Life: An American Interpretation* (New York: New American Library, 1951), p. 53.
11. From a paper presented at the 1957 Meeting of *The Mont Pelerin Society.*
12. Friedrich A. von Hayek, *The Constitution of Liberty* (Chicago: University of Chicago Press, 1960), p. 11.
13. Quoted by J. J. Spengler in "Machine-Made Justice and Some Implications," *Law and Contemporary Problems* (Durham: Duke University, Winter, 1963).

181

14. Hayek, *op. cit.*, p. 13.
15. *Ibid.*, p. 26, and chap. II, *passim*.
16. *Ibid.*, p. 19.
17. See Walter Bagehot, *Physics and Politics* (New York: Knopf, 1948), chap. 5: "It is a question whether the benevolence of mankind does more good than harm." This classic first appeared in 1869.
18. Simon Kuznets, *Modern Economic Growth: Rate, Structure and Spread* (New Haven: Yale University Press, 1966), pp. 421–26.
19. Alexis de Tocqueville, *Democracy in America* (New York: Harper & Row, 1966), pp. 279–80.
20. Shakespeare puts this eloquent defense of order into the mouth of Ulysses in *Troilus and Cressida,* Act I, scene iii.

CHAPTER 2

1. William Foote Whyte, *Street Corner Society* (Chicago: University of Chicago Press, 1943).
2. See below, pp. 55–56 and pp. 167 ff.
3. T. V. Smith, *The Ethics of Compromise and the Art of Containment* (Boston: Starr King Press, 1956).
4. Bertrand de Jouvenel, *De la Souveraineté* (Paris: Librairie de Médici, 1955).
5. T. V. Smith, *op. cit.*
6. The late Professor Willmoore Kendall used this term in "The Civil Rights Movement and the Coming Constitutional Crisis," *The Intercollegiate Review* (Philadelphia: Intercollegiate Society of Individualists, Inc., February–March, 1965), 1, No. 2, p. 54.
7. Quoted from a paper presented at the 1961 Meeting of *The Mont Pelerin Society.* In this paper the author, Professor Louis Rougier of Paris, made a sharp distinction between liberalism and democracy. "Liberalism is founded on the sovereignty of the human person and stands above the will of the majority . . . while democracy is founded on popular sovereignty and knows no higher law than the will of the majority." The absolute monarchs of the ancient regime, Rougier asserted, "would never have dared establish, as did the Republic, universal conscription, the law of suspects and hostages, the revolutionary wars to force peoples to be free, and in the process suppressing all individual guarantees, introducing total economic planning, militarizing the state and making terror a part of the governmental process, and ideological war an instrument of conquest." The First Republic, he concluded, "was the first totalitarian government in the history of Europe."
8. In *A Humane Economy: The Social Framework of the Free Market* (Chicago: Henry Regnery, 1960) William Roepke records a discussion of this issue with Benedetto Croce. Both were refugees from tyranny, Roepke from Hitler's Germany, Croce from Mussolini's Italy. Roepke argued that "any society, in all its aspects, is always a unit in which the

separate parts are interdependent and make up a whole which cannot be put together by arbitrary choice. . . . The economic order . . . must be understood as part of the total order of society and must correspond to the political and spiritual order. . . . Since liberty was indivisible, we could not have political and spiritual liberty without also choosing liberty in the economic field. . . . Conversely we had to be clear in our minds that a collectivist order meant the destruction of political and spiritual liberty. Therefore, the economy was in the front line of the defense of liberty and of all its consequences for the moral and humane pattern of our civilization." Croce rejected this argument. He held that "there was no necessary connection between political and spiritual freedom, on the one hand, and economic freedom on the other. Only the first mattered; economic freedom belonged to a lower and independent sphere where we could decide at will. In the economic sphere, the only question was one of expediency in the matter of organizing our economic life, and this question was not to be related with the decisive and incomparably higher question of political and spiritual freedom. The economic question was of no concern to the philosopher, who could be a liberal in the spiritual and political field and yet collectivist in the economic" (pp. 105–106).

9. In *The Democratic Way of Life, op. cit.*, T. V. Smith asserts that liberty and fraternity are impossible without a very considerable degree of equality, material as well as social. He recognizes that the drive for equality may be carried too far but relies on the spirit of sportsmanship to prevent this. He believes that the French revolutionaries were right in proclaiming liberty, fraternity and equality. Rougier, on the other hand (see note 7 above), agrees with Felix Morley that "equality strangled liberty, and fraternity passed swiftly into atrocity." Quoted from Morley's *The Power in the People* (New York: Van Nostrand, 1949). p. 155.

10. See below, p. 52 and pp. 56 ff.

11. *Democracy in America. op. cit.*, pp. 475–76.

12. *Ibid.*, p. 505.

13. *Ibid.*, pp. 505–506

14. *The New York Times*, September 9, 1912.

15. From Brandeis's dissenting opinion in *Olmstead v. U.S.*

16. Quoted by C. H. Bhabha, a former President of the Indian Banks' Association, in a speech delivered at the Bombay (India) Rotary Club on September 18, 1956, and issued in brochure form by the *Forum of Free Enterprise*, Bombay, India.

17. See above, note 8.

CHAPTER 3

1. I am indebted to the distinguished legal scholar Gustavo Velasco, Rector of the Escuela Libre de Derecho of Mexico City, for drawing my attention to this fact.

2. Quoted by Hayek, *op. cit.*, p. 165
3. B. Roscoe Pound, *An Introduction to the Philosophy of Law* (New Haven: Yale University Press, 1954), p. 7.
4. D. V. Cowen, *The Foundations of Freedom: Law and Government in South Africa* (Capetown: Oxford University Press, 1961), pp. 205–06.
5. *History* in *Great Books of the Western World* (Chicago: University of Chicago Press, 1952) VII, parag. 104, p. 233.
6. Thucydides, *The Peloponnesian War* (New York: The Modern Library, Random House, 1951), p. 104.
7. Edith Hamilton, *The Greek Way to Civilization* (New York: W. W. Norton, 1951), p. 23.
8. *Ibid.*, p. 7.
9. Quoted by Hayek, *op. cit.*, p. 57. See also Cowen, *op. cit.*, p. 208.
10. See Bruno Leoni, *Freedom and the Law* (New York: Van Nostrand, 1961), chap. 4, for an excellent account of the distinction between statute law and law as discovered by the Roman jurists, and for the importance the Romans attached to the long-run certainty which can be so conspicuously missing in statute law.
11. J. B. Bury, *History of the Later Roman Empire* (New York: Dover Publications, 1923) I, 13–14.
12. *Ibid.*, p. 14.
13. Lord Radcliffe, *The Problem of Power* (London: Secker & Warburg, 1952), pp. 20–21.
14. *Ibid.*, p. 21. For a clear account of the medieval concept of natural law, see Cowen, *op. cit.*, pp. 210–218.
15. Hayek, *op. cit.*, p. 19.
16. The passages from Locke cited in the text by paragraph numbers are from the J. W. Gough edition, Oxford, 1946.
17. Hayek, *op. cit.*, pp. 217–18.
18. *Ibid.*, 208 and note 10 above.
19. *Ibid.*, p. 103 and also the following: "Not only is liberty a system under which all government action is guided by principles, but it is an ideal which will not be preserved unless it is itself accepted as an over-riding principle governing all particular acts of legislation." Otherwise, Hayek continues, "though it may have to be temporarily infringed during a passing emergency . . . freedom is almost certain to be destroyed by piecemeal encroachments. For in each particular instance it will be possible to promise concrete and tangible advantages as a result of the curtailment of freedom while the benefits sacrificed will in their nature always be unknown and uncertain. . . . The promises which a free society has to offer can always be only chances and not certainties" (p. 68).
20. See *The Digest and General Report* on the discussions held at the colloquium of the International Association of Legal Scholars in Chicago in September 1957. See also Hayek, *op. cit.*, chap. 16.
21. See John Jewkes, *The New Ordeal by Planning: The Experience of the Forties and the Sixties* (London: Macmillan, 1968).
22. G. W. Keeton, *The Passing of Parliament* (London: Ernest Benn, Ltd., 1952), p. 23.

23. C. J. Hamson, *Executive Discretion and Judicial Control* (London: Stevenson & Sons, 1954), pp. 6 and 18–19. Professor Hamson prepared the General Report referred to in note 20 above. His lecture was given under a trust "to promote understanding among the common people . . . of the privileges which, in law and custom, they enjoy in comparison with other European peoples." Professor Hamson made it clear that in his opinion the situation mentioned in the trust no longer prevailed.

24. See *Address* by George Widner, reprinted in *The American Bar Association Journal* (July 1957).

25. The issue was discussed at some length at one of the meetings of the International Association of Legal Scholars referred to in note 20 above. Opinion was divided. All agreed, however, that the rule of law would be in jeopardy "if fundamental rights are substantially curtailed, or if delegated legislation is so prevalent as virtually to displace the legislative activity, or the functions of the Parliament." This quote is from *The Digest*. *The General Report* contained two significant passages: "To the ancient and continuing need to defend the individual against the State there should be added the need, especially in the Welfare-State type of community, of defending . . . the general interest against the drive of an organized group using legitimate power exclusively for its selfish interests. . . . In an apathetic or insufficiently vigilant society such a group could establish, and has . . . succeeded in establishing, a monopoly of power which involves a disruption of the institutions of the rule of law."

CHAPTER 4

1. K. C. Wheare, *Federal Government* (London: Oxford University Press, 1953).

2. Louis Rougier, *L'Erreur de la Démocratie Française* (Paris: Editions L'Esprit Nouveau, 1963), pp. 15–16.

3. See "The Federalist View of Federalism," by Martin Diamond in *Essays in Federalism* by Benton and others, published by The Institute for Studies in Federalism, Claremont Men's College, Claremont, California, 1961.

4. Quoted by J. Harry Cotton in *Royce on the Human Self* (Cambridge: Harvard University Press, 1954), pp. 259–60.

5. Quoted by Cowen, *op. cit.*, pp. 91–92.

6. John H. Stanbaugh, "How Democracy Dies," Study Paper No. 3 in *Task Force Studies in American Strategy and Strength* and reproduced in the *Congressional Record*, June 20, 1960.

7. The greatest weakness, as I see it, in Clarence Streit's magnificent plea for a larger federalism is his failure to recognize that a federation of socialist states is an impossibility. See his *Union Now: a Proposal for a Federal Union of the Democracies of the North Atlantic*, 15th ed., (New York: Harper & Bros., 1940).

8. I have mislaid the exact reference to this dictum of the most scholarly of the Founding Fathers.

9. Charles S. Hyneman, *The Supreme Court on Trial* (New York:

Atherton Press, 1963). See also Gottfried Dietz, *America's Political Dilemma: From Limited to Unlimited Democracy* (Baltimore: Johns Hopkins Press, 1968).

10. C. J. Bullock, "Direct Taxation Under the Constitution," *Political Science Quarterly,* 15, Nos., 2 & 3 (1900), pp. 228 ff.

11. In *Welfare and Taxation* (Oxford: Catholic School Guild, 1955) the eminent economist and statistician Colin Clark showed with convincing supporting evidence that the average British working-class family was paying appreciably more for welfare services—including education—than they could have bought them for in the open market.

12. *Messages and Papers of the Presidents* (New York: Bureau of National Literature, Inc., 1897).

13. Harry Kelvin, Jr., and Walter J. Blum, *The Uneasy Case for Progressive Taxation* (Chicago: University of Chicago Press, 1953).

14. See below, pp. 176–80.

15. *The New York Times,* March 3, 1930.

16. From a speech at the Illinois State Fair, August 4, 1952.

17. *The Future of Federalism* (Cambridge: Harvard University Press, 1962).

18. George C. S. Benson and Harold F. McClelland, *Consolidated Grants: A Means of Maintaining Fiscal Responsibility* (Washington: American Enterprise Association, December 1961). For similar recommendations see my *Planning for the South: An Inquiry into the Economics of Regionalism* (Nashville: Vanderbilt University Press, 1943), chapters VIII, IX, and X.

19. In a release dated April 1967 the Republican Coordinating Committee quoted Professor Roger A. Freeman of the Hoover Institute on War, Revolution and Peace as follows: "Though needs differ widely from state to state, and from area to area, it is national decisions on priorities which again and again determine what will be done, regardless of local needs or desires. . . . [Local governments] will almost always first determine what Federal money is available and then decide to act accordingly."

20. See above, p. 20.

21. The rest of this concluding passage from *Democracy in America, op. cit.,* (Vol. II, Part, 5 Chapter 6) is worth quoting here: "It provides for their security, foresees and supplies their necessities, facilitates their pleasures, manages their principal concerns, directs their industry, makes rules for their testaments, and divides their inheritances. . . . It covers the whole of social life with a network of petty, complicated rules that are both minute and uniform, through which even men of the greatest originality and the most vigorous temperament cannot force their heads above the crowd. It does not break men's will, but softens, bends and guides it; it seldom enjoins, but often inhibits action; it does not destroy anything, but prevents much being born; it is not at all tyrannical, but it hinders, restrains, enervates, stifles, and stultifies so much that in the end [the] nation is no more than a flock of timid and hardworking animals with the government as its shepherd."

CHAPTER 5

1. Joseph A. Schumpeter, *Capitalism, Socialism and Democracy,* 2nd ed. (New York: Harper & Bros., 1947), p. 67.
2. See Sumner H. Slichter, Harvard Graduate School of Business: The economy is becoming more competitive, not less so, and will continue to become more so" (*The Atlantic Monthly,* November 1949). George J. Stigler's careful quantitative investigations of the monopoly problem in the United States convinced him that competition had been on the increase since about 1900. See his *Five Lectures on Economic Problems* (New York: Macmillan & Co., 1950). Schumpeter, *op. cit.,* p. 84, asserted that capitalism operates "under a perennial gale of competition." Warren G. Nutter's findings in *The Extent of Enterprise Monopoly in the United States, 1899–1939* (Chicago: University of Chicago Press, 1951) confirmed Stigler's findings. John Kenneth Galbraith, in *The Affluent Society* (1958) and *The New Industrial State* (1967), both published by Houghton Mifflin (Boston), asserts with verve but with little supporting evidence that competition is a myth and that the consumer is no longer even a limited monarch.
3. See above, p. 5.
4. Masters of the spoken and written word with no direct responsibility for and no first-hand knowledge of practical affairs whose interest it is to work up and organize resentment, to nurse it, to voice it and to lead it. Schumpeter, *op. cit.,* p. 145.
5. Milton Friedman, "On Politics and Violence," *Newsweek,* June 24, 1968.
6. A. S. J. Baster, *The Little Less* (London: Methuen, 1947). In this delightful satire the author describes the conversion of the British economy between the two world wars into a caricature of a competitive economy as the government encouraged output restrictions in one activity after another.
7. Adam Smith presented this argument in *The Theory of Moral Sentiments* (London: 1759) 17 years before the appearance of his *Wealth of Nations.*
8. Henry Hazlitt, *The Foundations of Morality* (New York: Van Nostrand, 1964), p. 333.
9. I have borrowed here freely from *Planning for the South, op. cit.,* pp. 17–20.
10. Chicago: University of Chicago Press, 1942. A second edition appeared in 1965.
11. Pitrim A. Sorokin, *Social and Cultural Dynamics* (New York. American Book Co., 1937). His index covers eight major European countries and eight and a quarter centuries. It takes into account the duration of wars, size of forces involved, number of killed and wounded, the number of countries involved, and the proportion of combatants to total populations involved.
12. Eugene Staley, *War and the Foreign Investor: A Study in the Relations*

of *International Politics and International Investment* (Garden City, New York: Doubleday, Doran, 1935). See also Karl Polanyi, *The Great Transformation: The Political and Economic Origins of Our Time* (New York: Rinehart & Co., 1944), chap. 1, "The Hundred Years' Peace." The author was referring to the period 1815–1914. "The nineteenth century produced a phenomenon unheard of in the annals of Western civilization, a hundred years' peace" (p. 5), an "almost miraculous performance" (p. 6). Polanyi is concerned here with wars between major powers. "A computation of comparable figures for the two preceding centuries gives an average of sixty to seventy years of major wars in each" (p. 5).

13. See Max Weber, *General Economic History* (New York: Collier Books edition, 1961): "In the last resort the factor which produced capitalism is the rational permanent enterprise, rational accounting, rational technology and rational law, but again not these alone. Necessary complementary factors were the rational spirit, the rationalization of the conduct of life in general, and a rationalistic economic ethic" (p. 260). This is a translation by Frank H. Knight of lectures delivered by Max Weber in the winter of 1919–1920.

14. *Capitalism, Socialism and Democracy, op. cit.*

CHAPTER 6

1. From at least the time of Adam Smith, economists have recognized the need for public interventions to correct market imperfections of the sort here under discussion. A. C. Pigou's *The Economics of Welfare* (London: Macmillan, 1920) is a classic. For a time the inability of market forces to equate benefits and burdens seemed to him to point to some form of democratic socialism as the ideal. Professor Galbraith makes much of this imperfection in the books cited in note 2 in the preceding chapter.

2. For penetrating discussions of the pitfalls involved in handling what I have called "the responsibility principle" (also referred to as the problem of "neighborhood effects"), see R. H. Coase, "The Problem of Social Cost," *The Journal of Law and Economics* (October 1960); G. H. Peters, *Cost-Benefit Analysis* (London: Institute of Economic Affairs, 1966); J. M. Stepp and H. H. Macaulay, *The Pollution Problem* (Washington: American Enterprise Institute for Public Policy Research, 1968). By the mid-1950s Pigou had regretfully admitted that planners "seldom knew enough to decide in what fields and to what extent the State, on account of [the gap between public and private costs] could usefully interfere with individual freedom of choice." Quoted by Hayek, *op. cit.*, p. 492.

3. Coase, *op. cit.*

4. E. Mishan, *The Costs of Growth* (London: Staples, 1967).

5. *The Wealth of Nations, op. cit.*, p. 446.

6. See *Reclaiming the American Dream* (New York: Random House, 1965), chapter 5: "The key to our system, lost in the twentieth century,

was a third sector, neither commercial not governmental, which solved most public problems."

7. See above, p. 28. Also James M. Buchanan, *The Public Finances: An Introductory Text Book* (Homewood: Richard D. Irwin, Inc., 1960), pp. 467–73.

8. See "Tyranny in the Internal Revenue Service," and "Time for Reform in the IRS" in the August 1967 and September 1968 issues of *Reader's Digest.*

9. In *The Communist Manifesto* Marx recommended ten measures for undermining the bourgeois social structure and preparing the way for the Communist takeover. "A heavy progressive or graduated tax" on personal incomes was the second of these recommendations.

10. See below, pp. 170–80.

CHAPTER 7

1. See above, p. 67.

2. Schumpeter, *op. cit.*

3. *National Party Platforms,* compiled by Kirk H. Porter and Donald Bruce Johnson (Urbana: University of Illinois Press, 1966).

4. See Wilson E. Schmidt, "Public Policy and the Foreign Sector," in *New Arguments in Economics,* edited by Helmut Schoecht and James W. Wiggin (New York: Van Nostrand, 1963), pp. 107–130.

5. Boston: Little, Brown & Co., and the Atlantic Monthly Press, 1937, pp. 213–14. More recently Professor William Roepke stressed the same point: "The last thing we desire is a world of wandering nomads. . . . The greatest possible number of men should have the freedom to move, but only the smallest possible number the desire to use it, because they live under conditions of life and work which make most of them happy if they stay where they are, even if they have to accept a smaller money income. . . . It is not natural for the common man to leave his home and his country and to try his luck elsewhere in a strange climate, among strange people often speaking another language. See his article, "Barriers to Immigration" in *Twentieth Century Economic Thought,* Glenn E. Hoover, editor (New York: Philosophical Library, 1950), p. 643.

6. The National Planning Board, *Problems of a Changing Population* (Washington: Government Printing Office, 1938), p. 63.

7. Philadelphia: University of Pennsylvania Press, 1936: "Though there may be hope of reorganizing the rural life of the area," Goodrich continued, "and though we may expect some continuation of the southward drift of manufacturing, these changes hold out to the region no prospect of an increase in opportunity great enough to remove its long-standing deficiencies, to care for the population now in distress, and to counteract the effect of a high birth rate" (p. 441).

8. Echoing the Goodrich analysis, the Board, in *Problems of a Changing Population, op. cit.,* saw "little support for a belief that opportunities for part-time or full-time industrial employment can be widely distributed geographically in the near future. The record of both past

migration and of industrial expansion show that workers have usually moved to the factory, rather than the factory to the workers" (pp. 71–72).

9. Reworking census figures for the period 1899–1937, Professor J. J. Spengler predicted that "a considerable proportion of such future manufacturing as takes place in the United States will take place . . . in the Southeast." "Regional Differences and the Future of Manufacturing in America," *Southern Economic Journal*, 7, No. 4 (1941), p. 488. Factual and theoretical reasoning in support of the position defended here will be found in *Planning for the South*, *op. cit.*, especially chapter 8. For confirmation of Spengler's prediction see James G. Maddox *et al.*, *The Advancing South: Manpower, Prospects and Problems* (New York: Twentieth Century Fund, 1967).

CHAPTER 8

1. Sumner H. Slichter, *The American Economy: Its Problems and Prospects* (New York: Knopf, 1948), p. 7.
2. An excellent brief account of the origin, accomplishments, and demise of the NRA will be found in Merle Fainsod *et al.*, *Government and the American Economy* (New York: W. W. Norton, 1959), chapter 17.
3. *Schechter v. U.S.*, 295 495.
4. That this is not an unsupported dictum of the author, see Milton Friedman's "Because or Despite," *Newsweek* (October 28, 1968), p. 104. "There is no doubt," Professor Friedman writes, "that the condition of the ordinary man improved greatly in the past 35 years. There is no doubt that a vast array of legislation was adopted in that period with the announced aim of improving the condition of the ordinary man. Is it not obvious that the first must be the consequence of the second? Far from it. . . . The mere fact that one event precedes or accompanies another does not demonstrate that the one causes the other—*post hoc ergo propter hoc* is the label for a logical fallacy, not a valid method of reasoning. . . . The condition of the ordinary man has improved greatly in the past 35 years—as it did in the prior 35 years and in the 35 years before that. The improvement has throughout . . . been a product of the enormous opportunities provided to all by a competitive free enterprise system—the most effective machine yet developed for eliminating poverty and raising the standard of life of the the masses. The recent improvement has occurred despite a mass of ill-considered and mischievous legislation. It will continue even if that legislation is retained. But it would proceed more rapidly and its benefits would be spread wider if that legislation were repealed."
5. Ray Marshall, "Some Factors Influencing the Growth of Unions in the South," *Industrial Relations Research Association Proceedings*, 1961, pp. 166 ff.
6. See Thomas O'Hanlon, "The Case Against the Unions,'" *Fortune*, January 1968: "Once a catalyst of social change, the union movement has become a stronghold of discrimination against Negroes" (p. 3).

The investigations of professors Vernon M. Briggs and F. Ray Marshall, as reported in *The Wall Street Journal*, October 16, 1967, revealed that in five craft unions (Plumbers, Electricians, Iron Workers, Carpenters and Sheet Metal Workers) in selected Northern areas in 1965 less than 2.5 percent of 5,908 apprentices were Negroes.

7. Herbert C. Morton in *Public Contracts and Private Wages* (Washington: Brookings Institution, 1965) and Carrol L. Christenson and Richard A. Myren in *Wage Policy Under the Walsh-Healey Public Contracts Act* (Bloomington: Indiana University Press, 1966) all recommended that the act be repealed. Christenson and Myren noted that the act undercuts the government's efforts "to keep high-wage unions from scoring inordinate gains" (note 16, p. 226). The regional protectionism inherent in the act is emphasized in my *The Walsh-Healey Public Contracts Act* (New York: American Enterprise Association, 1952): "In fiscal 1950 ... firms in the 11 states of the Southeast received only 7.25 percent of Walsh-Healey contracts by number and 4.6 percent by value despite the fact that 21 percent of our total population resided in these states and that firms located in these states were responsible for 13 percent of total wages and salaries earned in 1950" (pp. 28–29).

8. O. R. Strackbein, *The Prevailing Minimum Wage* (Washington: Graphics Arts Press, 1939), p. 65. The author of this eulogy of the Fair Labor Standards Act was long active in Washington as a lobbyist for businesses seeking protection from foreign competition.

9. For details see my "Geographical Aspects of a Minimum Wage," *Harvard Business Review*, Spring, 1946, p. 293.

10. In the above-mentioned article it was noted that in the first quarter of 1945 when the Administration was urging that the minimum wage be increased from 40 to 65 cents an hour, 42 percent of all employees in Tennessee engaged in manufacturing were receiving less than 65 cents an hour; that in the apparel industry the figure was 93 percent; in textiles 92 percent; in furniture 83.5 percent. There were only six industry groups in which no employees were paid less than 65 cents an hour and these were either highly unionized or were war industries working on cost-plus contracts and under Walsh-Healey wage determinations.

11. James E. Blair, "Regarding the Minimum Wage," *The Freeman*, July 1965. Yale Brozen, *Automation and Jobs* (Graduate School of Business, University of Chicago, *Selected Papers*, No. 18). Yale Brozen and Milton Friedman, *The Minimum Wage: Who Pays?* (Washington: Free Society Association, 1966). Marshall R. Colberg, "Minimum Wage Effects on Florida's Economic Development," *Journal of Law and Economics*, October 1960. D. E. Kaun, "Minimum Wages, Factor Substitution and the Marginal Producer," *Quarterly Journal of Economics*, August 1965. G. Macesich and C. T. Stewart, Jr., "Recent Department of Labor Studies of Minimum Wage Effects," *Southern Economic Journal*, April 1960. John Peterson, "Employment Effects of Minimum Wages," *Journal of Political Economy*, October 1957. See also Harold Demitz, "Minorities in the Market Place," *North Carolina Law Review*, February 1965.

12. Michael Harrington, *The Other America: Poverty in the United States* (New York: Macmillan, 1963).
13. *Report of the National Advisory Commission on Civil Disorders* (New York: Bantam Books, 1968), p. 420.
14. W. Allen Wallis, "Commitment, Concern and Apathy," *The Freeman* (January 1968), p. 10. This article is from an address given by Dr. Wallis on September 21, 1967, before the National Conference of Christians and Jews in New York City.
15. Quoted by Henry Hazlitt in *Newsweek* (April 11, 1966), p. 90.
16. *Ibid.*
17. Henry C. Simons, *Economic Policy for a Free Society* (Chicago: University of Chicago Press, 1948), pp. 121–22.

CHAPTER 9

1. B. Roscoe Pound, *The Legal Immunities of Labor Unions* (Washington: American Enterprise Association, 1957), p. 21.
2. See *passim* in the chapter "Some Reflections on Syndicalism" in Simons, *op. cit.*
3. See above, p. 95.
4. Sumner H. Slichter in *The Commercial and Financial Chronicle*, July 23, 1959.
5. Slichter, *ibid.*
6. F. A. Harper, *Why Wages Rise* (Irvington-on-Hudson: Foundation for Economic Education, 1957).
7. Sidney Weintraub, "A Law that Cannot be Repealed," *Challenge* (New York University, April 1962), p. 18. See also the following from "Materials Prepared for the Joint Committee on the Economic Report of the President" and published under the title *Productivity, Prices and Income* (85th Cong., 1st Sess. Washington: Government Printing Office, 1957): "One of the most important generalizations suggested by this study is that over the long run . . . the share of total income going to labor and to nonlabor categories has remained about the same."
8. This section borrows freely from Milton Friedman, *Capitalism and Freedom* (Chicago: University of Chicago Press, 1962), pp. 137–60, who in turn acknowledges his indebtedness to Walter Gelhorn, *Individual Freedom and Government Restraint* (Baton Rouge: Louisiana State University Press, 1955).
9. In *Economics of the Colour Bar* (London: Institute of Economic Affairs, 1964), W. H. Hutt, at the time Dean of the Faculty of Commerce of the University of Cape Town, South Africa, showed how effectively the imposition of a high minimum wage and collective bargaining protected the whites of South Africa and contributed to the present impasse there. Prior to these developments private competitive enterprise was demonstrating what the fundamentalist Boers had always denied: that the Negro was capable of doing more than hew wood and carry water.
10. See above, pp. 107–09 and note 10 to chapter 8, and pp. 166–67 below.

CHAPTER 10

1. Defined as the ratio of children under five years of age per 1,000 women of child-bearing age.
2. *16th Census of Population.* Release of February 21, 1941. Series P–5, No. 4.
3. These figures were supplied by Don Paarlberg, Hillenbrand Professor of Agricultural Economics, Purdue University, in a letter dated February 17, 1967.
4. Dr. Kermit Gordon cited this fact in an article in the *Saturday Review* (January 1965), and spoke of the "strange workings" of an aid program that gave most to those needing it least.
5. From a U.S. Department of Agriculture Farm Release reproduced in The Elston Bank and Trust Company (Crawfordsville, Indiana) *Farm Letter,* December 1965.
6. Milton Friedman, "Foreign Economic Aid," *The Yale Review* (Summer, 1958). For a more recent description of the many ways in which our fear of international competition has produced policies that have hurt the people in the underdeveloped countries, see Peter B. Kenan, *International Economics,* 2nd ed., (Englewood Cliffs, New Jersey: Prentice-Hall, 1967), pp. 104–05. Professor Kenan is the Director of the International Economic Workshop, Columbia University.
7. B. R. Shenoy, "Why India Starves," *Barron's* (October 5, 1964). Professor Shenoy is the Director of the School of Social Sciences, Gujarat University, Ahmedabad, India, and a member of the Mont Pelerin Society. For a more cautious endorsement of Professor Shenoy's indictment, see Kenan, *op. cit.:* "The United States imposes import quotas on wheat, rye, cotton and other major staples in order to defend its domestic support prices against foreign competition. . . . [It then] sells its farm surpluses to the less developed countries on terms that may hurt competing producers and may even injure the recipient countries. Under the Food for Peace program, the United States government sells surplus wheat and other farm products for foreign currencies rather than dollars, allowing the less developed countries to increase their food imports without using up their precious export earnings. The program has been praised as warding off famine in countries with food deficits (especially India), but has sometimes been accused of reducing the food exports of other low-income countries and of causing the recipient countries to rely on U.S. food, rather than developing their own food production. This last charge, if true, is a grave indictment" (p. 104).

CHAPTER 11

1. In an article entitled "Voluntary Social Security," in *The Wall Street Journal* (December 20, 1966) James M. Buchanan and Colin D. Campbell, of the departments of economics at the University of Virginia and Dartmouth College, respectively, estimated the deficit prior to the 1965

liberalizing amendments at $325 billion, and at least $400 billion at the end of calendar year 1966.

2. *Ibid.*
3. Frank G. Dickinson, "The Social Insurance Principle," *The Journal of Insurance* (Fall–Winter, 1960), p. 3.
4. Jerry E. Bishop in *The Wall Street Journal* (August 15, 1968).
5. *Ibid.*
6. William H. Beveridge and others, *Tariffs: The Case Examined* (London: Longmans, 1931), pp. 239–40.
7. *Full Employment in a Free Society* (New York: W. W. Norton, 1954).
8. Philip D. Bradley, *Involuntary Participation in Unionism* (Washington: American Enterprise Institute, 1956).
9. Quoted in an article in *U.S. News and World Report* (July 17, 1967).
10. *Ibid.*
11. F. O. Jacobs, "Welfare Crisis: Subsidy for Separation," *The Wall Street Journal* (July 22, 1968).
12. *U.S. News and World Report* (July 17, 1967).

CHAPTER 12

1. London: Macmillan, 1936. The citations in the text are from the 1954 reprint.
2. *The Economic Consequences of the Peace* (New York: Harcourt, Brace & Howe, 1920).
3. Thus, at the very end of *The General Theory* (pp. 383–84) we find this much quoted reference to the power of ideas: "Ideas . . . both when they are right and when they are wrong, are more powerful than is commonly understood. Indeed the world is ruled by little else. Practical men, who believe themselves to be quite exempt from any intellectual influences, are usually the slaves of some defunct economist. Madmen in authority, who hear voices in the air, are distilling their frenzy from some academic scribbler of a few years back. I am sure that the power of vested interests is vastly exaggerated compared with the gradual encroachment of ideas. . . . Sooner or later, it is ideas, not vested interests, which are dangerous for good or ill."
4. See the Introduction as it appears in H. D. Henderson, *Supply and Demand* (London: Pitman Publishing Co., 1921).
5. Charles Gide and Charles Rist, *History of Economic Thought* (Boston: D. C. Heath & Co., 1948) p. 739.
6. I am indebted to Gottfried Haberler for recalling to my attention this document (*Economic Stability in the Postwar World*) and the late Alexander Loveday's role in its formulation. Haberler was too modest to mention that his own thinking on the problem of the business cycle may also have influenced the report. His classic, *Prosperity and Depression* (Geneva: League of Nations, 1937), was written while he was attached to the Financial Section of the League of Nations under a Rockefeller grant.

7. For a fuller discussion of the bill, see my "Regional Aspects of Full Employment," *The Southern Economic Journal* (July 1946).
8. Oskar Morgenstern, "Qui Numerare Incipit Errare Incipit," *Fortune* (October 1963), pp. 142 ff.
9. *The Wall Street Journal,* January 27, 1968.
10. See chapter 8, note 9.
11. The Chase Manhattan Bank, *World Business* (October 1968), p. 9.
12. An analogy used by Professor Gottfried Haberler.
13. See above, p. 91.
14. *The Economic Journal* (June 1946). The article appeared after Keynes's death.

CHAPTER 13

1. Willmoore Kendall, *op. cit.,* p. 94.
2. *Capitalism and Freedom, op. cit.,* pp. 192 ff.
3. *Ibid.,* p. 193, note.
4. *Ibid.,* p. 192.
5. See chapter 6, note 1.
6. Chicago: University of Chicago Press, 1944, p. 210.
7. See chapter 8, note 14. See also the discussion of the problem in Van Sickle and Rogge, *op. cit.:* "It would be quite easy to imagine a broad security program of admirable simplicity. The government might, for example, issue weekly or monthly checks to all families in the United States, based on the requirements for a really Spartan existence. The only condition for eligibility would be the submission each year of a detailed family income tax declaration. The government would then levy a progressive income tax, which, in the case of each family, would begin with the amount received over and above the family annuity. Thus each family would be assured of a tax-free minimum income, which would vary with the size of the family. The income tax admittedly would have to be heavy, but while we are allowing free play to our imaginations, we can also imagine some substantial savings: no more public works undertaken just for the sake of providing employment; no more minimum wage and maximum hour laws; no more restrictive union agreements; no more agricultural price supports and acreage restriction programs; no more special programs for the needy aged, for dependent children, for the blind and physically handicapped; no more tariffs to protect high-cost enterprises" (pp. 522 23).
8. See above, pp. 79–81.
9. See above, p. 105.
10. See above, p. 105.

APPENDIX

1. This note elaborates on an article by the author in *The Wabash Alumni Bulletin* (April 1962), pp. 14 ff.

Index

Numbers in italics refer to chapters. When reference is made to notes, the page number is followed by a colon, the chapter number is in italics, and the number of the note is in Arabic numerals.

197